JumpStarters

100 GAMES

TO SPARK DISCUSSIONS

Group LOVELAND, COLORADO

Group's R.E.A.L. Guarantee to you:

Every Group resource incorporates our R.E.A.L. approach to ministry—a unique philosophy that results in long-term retention and life transformation. It's ministry that's:

This is EARL. He's R.E.A.L mixed up. (Get it?)

Relational
Because student-to-student interaction enhances learning and builds Christian friendships.

Experiential
Because what students experience sticks with them up to 9 times longer than what they simply hear or read.

Applicable
Because the aim of Christian education is to be both hearers and doers of the Word.

Learner-based
Because students learn more and retain it longer when the process is designed according to how they

JumpStarters: 100 Games to Spark Discussions

Visit our Web site: **www.grouppublishing.com**

Credits

Contributing Authors: Katrina Arbuckle, Tim Baker, Michael W. Capps, Steve Case, Monica Kay Glenn, Stacy Haverstock, Michele Howe, Mikal Keefer, Trish Kline, Pamela Malloy, Teresa McCasland, Martha Menne, Janet Dodge Narum, Todd Outcalt, Christina Schofield, and Donna K. Stearns
Editor: Amy Simpson
Creative Development Editor: Jim Kochenburger
Chief Creative Officer: Joani Schultz
Copy Editor: Lyndsay E. Bierce
Designer and Art Director: Jean Bruns
Cover Art Director: Jeff A. Storm
Cover Designer: Ray Tollison
Cover Photography: Stone
Computer Graphic Artist: Stephen Beer
Illustrator: Paula Becker
Production Manager: Dodie Tipton

Unless otherwise noted, Scripture taken from the HOLY BIBLE, NEW INTERNATIONAL VERSION®. Copyright © 1973, 1978, 1984 by International Bible Society. Used by permission of Zondervan Publishing House. All rights reserved.

Library of Congress Cataloging-in-Publication Data

JumpStarters : 100 games to spark discussions / [contributing authors, Katrina Arbuckle ... et al. ; editor, Amy Simpson].
    p. cm.
   Includes indexes.
   ISBN 0-7644-2219-7 (alk. paper)
   1. Church group work with teenagers. 2. Games in Christian education. I. Arbuckle, Katrina. II. Simpson, Amy.

BV4447 .J86 2001
268'.443--dc21

                                      00-057813

10 9 8 7 6 5 4 3 2   10 09 08 07 06 05 04 03 02 01
Printed in the United States of America.

CONTENTS

TITLE	TOPIC	PAGE

JUMPSTARTERS

CONTENTS

J
U
M
P
S
T
A
R
T
E
R
S

I
N
T
R
O

This book is full of games—100 games your teenagers will love—from relays to brainteasers to silly twists on old favorites.

But that's not all! Each game is also a discussion starter. Games relate to a variety of important, relevant topics, such as worship, peer pressure, dating, the Bible, stress, and God's love.

Use the games by themselves, or use the accompanying questions and suggested Scripture passages to launch discussions and connect to Bible lessons. To find the game you need, check out the Scripture and topic indexes on pages 109-110.

Use these games to help your teenagers have fun, to capture their attention, and to help them evaluate important topics. *Jump Starters: 100 Games to Spark Discussions* may be just the resource you need to help your fun-loving young people learn more about faith in everyday life.

A Little Better All the Time

TOPIC: *Hope*

SCRIPTURE: *Romans 5:1-5; 2 Corinthians 4:18*

SUPPLIES: *paper, pens or pencils*

Have youth sit in a circle. Give each person one sheet of paper and a pen or pencil. If your group is large, have participants form smaller groups of eight to ten and play the game in their smaller groups.

At the top of the paper, have each person secretly write a sentence about someone in high school. Teenagers should give their characters names, and their sentences should talk about something lousy that happened to their characters during the day. For example, a person might write, "Rose dropped her tray in the lunchroom and everyone laughed," "Tom forgot his homework," or "Jackie saw her boyfriend kissing another girl in the hall."

When participants have written their sentences, have them pass their papers one person to the right. Those people should read the sentences and each add another sentence about how the situations got just a little better. When the second sentences have been written, have those authors fold the papers under the first sentences so only the second sentences are exposed. Then participants should pass the papers on again.

Have participants read the exposed sentences and write new sentences that again make the situations a little better. They should fold the papers again so only their sentences show, then pass the papers along.

Continue in this manner until the papers arrive back at their original positions. Then have teenagers unfold the papers and share their stories of how things went from lousy to great.

DISCUSSION

• What does this old saying mean: "When it rains it pours"?
• What makes you feel better when you have a bad day?
• When have you given up hope and then seen things get better?
• Where does hope come from?
• How can hope change our lives?

All Tied Up

TOPIC: *Prayer*

SCRIPTURE: *Matthew 6:6-13*

SUPPLIES: *several rolls of plastic wrap, a stopwatch*

Have youth form four teams. Give each team a roll of plastic wrap. Instruct each team to tightly wrap one member with the plastic wrap from head (not face) to toe. The wrapped member's arms should be down at his or her sides, and the wrap should inhibit movement of any kind. Each team should use the same amount of plastic wrap.

When you say go, teams will unwrap their wrapped members as quickly as possible. Time each team and then repeat the game, challenging the teams to try to improve their times.

DISCUSSION

- When we're struggling with problems, how can prayer help us and set us free from worry?
- When have you been "tied up" with lack of faith and fear, even though you knew God was ready to meet your needs?
- What are some ways we can equip ourselves for effective prayer?
- How does Satan try to discourage us from meeting with God in prayer?

Anatomy Quiz

TOPIC: *The Church*

SCRIPTURE: *1 Corinthians 12:12*

SUPPLIES: *paper, pens or pencils*

This game appears to be a no-brainer, but it's a little more challenging than it seems. The object is to list ten body parts that have only three letters. (Crude or slang terms don't count.) Three of the parts begin with vowels, and the remaining seven begin with consonants.

Have youth form teams. Give each team paper and pens or pencils, and see which team can come up with the correct answers the fastest! Try it yourself before you peek at the answers in the margin.

DISCUSSION

• What do all ten of these things have in common?
• How do these body parts function together?
• How are the body parts similar to the church?
• How does the church relate to the different body parts?
• If one part is missing, how does that affect the body? the church?

Armageddon

TOPIC: *Violence*

SCRIPTURE: *Philippians 2:13-15*

SUPPLIES: *at least 16 foam balls of any size, aluminum foil, transparent tape, masking tape, a strobe light*

Before this game, cover the foam balls with aluminum foil. Secure the foil with transparent tape. Use masking tape to mark a line down the middle of the playing area.

Have youth form two teams. Divide the foil-covered balls between the two teams. Point out the dividing line you marked down the middle of the playing area, and highlight any boundaries or obstacles in the room.

LEADER TIP
While it's always a
challenge to hit a
moving target, the
strobe light and
the foil add to the
adventure. To
make this game
even more excit-
ing, add black
lights, and spray
some of the balls
with glow-in-the-
dark paint. Have all the participants wear black clothing and white
gloves. Also, take note that strobe lights have been known to trig-
ger seizures in people with epilepsy. If this may cause a problem
for one of your students, use a black light instead.

Tell teams the object of the game is for teams to throw the foam balls at each other. If a ball hits a person, that person is out of the game and should sit on the floor at the spot he or she was hit until the game ends. The team with the last person standing wins.

Turn off the lights, turn on the strobe light, and have youth play several rounds.

DISCUSSION

- What was it like to be a target in this game?
- What was it like to try to hit a moving target?
- How does this game relate to the violence in today's world?
- What causes the violence we see around us?
- What are the consequences of violence?

Awesome Love

TOPIC: *God's Love*

SCRIPTURE: *1 Corinthians 13:4-13*

SUPPLIES: *newsprint or dry erase board, markers, timer or stopwatch, Bibles*

Have youth form groups of four. Give each person a Bible and instruct participants to find 1 Corinthians 13. Tell groups that they'll have sixty seconds to choose one aspect of love described in 1 Corinthians 13 and think of a scene that depicts a practical way God shows us that aspect of love. For example, if a group chooses "love protects," the group must come up with a scene that shows how God protects us. They may plan a scene of teenagers driving in a car on a rainy night with angels overhead.

After the sixty seconds of planning time, each group has two minutes to draw its scene. When time is up, the other groups must try to guess which aspect of love the group was trying to depict. Have groups take turns displaying their pictures while other groups guess. You may want to repeat the activity until you've covered all the aspects of love described in 1 Corinthians 13.

DISCUSSION

- What are some ways you sense the love of God around you each day?
- How can we become instruments for God to use in loving others?
- In what ways does God's love for us differ from the world's idea of love?
- How can we learn to trust God's love for us even when it doesn't make sense to us?

Balancing Our Faith

TOPIC: *Sharing Faith*

SCRIPTURE: *Romans 1:13-16*

SUPPLIES: *1 baseball cap and 1 balloon per team of 5 or 6*

Have youth form teams of five or six, and give each team one baseball cap and one balloon. Have each team select one person to be the first to put on the baseball cap and balance the balloon on the peak of the cap. The object of the game is for a person from each team to walk to a point approximately ten feet away and back to the team without allowing the balloon to fall off the hat or touching it with any part of the body. The person then passes the hat and balloon to

the next person on the team, who must complete the same action. (Participants can use their hands to pass the hat and balloon to the next player.) Challenge the students to try to finish the relay as quickly as possible.

DISCUSSION
- How is balancing the balloon similar to sharing our faith with the world?
- How do we sometimes "drop" opportunities to share our faith?
- What happens when we "drop" an opportunity to share with someone?
- Once we pass our faith on to someone else, how can we support that person?

Bargains Are Us

TOPIC: *Stewardship*
SCRIPTURE: *Romans 12:1, 6-8*
SUPPLIES: *6 new inexpensive products such as a box of soap powder, a can of corn, a new sponge, nail polish remover, a box of light bulbs, and a can of coffee; record of prices for all items; table*

Before the game, record the price of each item and remove the price tags from all the products. Display all the products on a table.

Tell participants that each person has twenty-five dollars to spend. Contestants must choose the products (and the quantity of each) they think they can purchase with their money. They can purchase more than one of each product on the table. The person who comes closest to twenty-five dollars without going over wins.

After participants have chosen their products, reveal the prices, and calculate which person came closest to twenty-five dollars without going over. For example, a person may choose ten cans of corn, two boxes of soap powder, one sponge, two boxes of light bulbs, and two bottles of nail polish remover. You then reveal that the cost of the corn is $.79 per can, the soap powder is $4.69 per box, the sponge is $1.59, the light bulbs are $1.99 per box, and the nail polish remover is $.99 per bottle. The person's total would come to $24.83.

- What does it mean to be a good steward?
- What are the consequences of being a good steward with money?
- Read Romans 12:1, 6-8. Besides money, what else should we be good stewards of?
- Why is stewardship important to God?
- How is stewardship an act of worship?

Beard of Cheese

TOPIC : *Temptation*

SCRIPTURE : *2 Timothy 2:22*

SUPPLIES : *duct tape, bags of puffy cheese-flavored snacks, bowls*

Have youth form teams of five to six. Have each team designate one participant to "grow a beard." To begin, have players wrap duct tape, sticky side out, around their chosen player's head, beginning under the nose and wrapping only the lower part of the face (leaving the mouth free).

When each team has wrapped its delegate, distribute a bowl of puffy cheese-flavored snacks to each group. Instruct groups that when you say "go," each team should begin applying cheese snacks

to the sticky beard, racing to see who can build the best beard of cheese in the shortest time.

DISCUSSION

• Why might a beard of cheese be a bad idea for someone who is dieting? How is that like the temptations to sin that we face?
• What is the best way to avoid sinning?
• What sorts of situations subject us to temptation?
• How can you stay far from temptation without isolating yourself from your peers?

Befriended

TOPIC: *Friendship*
SCRIPTURE: *Mark 1:16-20*
SUPPLIES: *assorted stickers*

Have teenagers form two groups. Place a sticker on the back of each person in the first group. Then give a few people in this group extra stickers, which they should hold in their hands. Everyone else in this group should pretend they have stickers in their hands. Tell the second group (those without stickers) that they must try to keep the people in the first group from placing stickers on their backs.

Begin the game, allowing the first group to chase the second group, putting stickers on their backs, or pretending to do so.

Once the first group has given away all its extra stickers, stop the game. The players from the second group who now have stickers on their backs become part of the first group.

Repeat the game until everyone has been "stickered" into one group.

DISCUSSION

• What was it like to "sticker" other people into your group?
• What was it like to be "accepted" into a new group?
• Read Mark 1:16-20. How can Jesus calling the disciples be seen as a gesture of friendship?

- How do you think the disciples felt to be accepted into a new group?
- What can we learn about friendship from Jesus' calling of the disciples?
- What signs of friendship might help us be better friends to one another?

Belly Ball

TOPIC: *Justice*
SCRIPTURE: *Matthew 20:1-16*
SUPPLIES: *beach ball, masking tape, large empty trash can*

Using masking tape, create a line on the floor for participants to stand behind. Place a large empty trash can several feet in front of this line. Have the group form two teams.

Tell participants that in this game, each player will stand behind the line and try to make a basket in the trash can by bouncing the beach ball off his or her belly. The team with the most baskets will win.

After teams play the game once, tell participants they're going to play again. This time, all the girls can shoot the basket normally, while boys continue bouncing the ball off their stomachs.

DISCUSSION
- How did you feel when I told you the girls were allowed to use their hands to make a basket?
- What are some things in life you feel are unfair?
- Read Matthew 20:1-16. In what ways has God demonstrated that he is fair and just?
- Have you ever felt like the first shift workers in this passage, frustrated with God for something that seemed to be unfair?
- How has God shown grace to you by giving you something you didn't deserve?

Blackout

TOPIC: *Money/Materialism*

SCRIPTURE: *1 Timothy 6:17-19*

SUPPLIES: *lots of loose change, 1 flashlight per 2 students*

B efore this game, hide coins all over the playing area.
As students arrive, ask them to find partners. Give each pair a flashlight. Turn off all the lights, and give players several minutes to find all the change they can. The pair with the most change at the end of that time wins the game.

DISCUSSION

• How does this game mirror the way many people live?

• What sort of people are you impressed by? What sort of people do you try to impress?

• Why are we often impressed by wealth?

• Is it a sin to be rich? Explain.

• How can wealth be used to glorify God?

• How can we be good stewards of the money we receive?

• What can we do to make sure money never becomes too important to us?

Bland Leading the Bland

TOPIC: *Compassion*

SCRIPTURE: *Job 2:12-13; 6:6-7*

SUPPLIES: *a variety of "bland" foods (such as cooked rice, cooked egg whites, cream of rice, and raw tofu), covered bowls, paper, pens or pencils, enough plastic spoons per person to have one spoon per food, blindfolds, candy bars or some other flavorful prize (optional)*

B efore the game, prepare the foods, and place them in covered bowls where no one will see them.
Give each person paper, a pen or pencil, and a plastic spoon. Have players sit in a circle and put on blindfolds. Pass one bowl of food around the circle. After each student has tried the food, put the bowl

away. Collect the spoons. Then allow players to remove their blind-folds and write down their guesses as to what the food was. Then distribute clean plastic spoons. Have players blindfold themselves again, and pass around another bowl of food. Continue until you've passed around all the foods, giving players clean spoons for each food.

After all the foods have been tasted, reveal the identity of each food and see who got the most right. You may want to give all the students candy bars (or something else with a lot of flavor) to finish off the game.

DISCUSSION

- What is compassion?
- Read Job 2:12-13. Why would Job compare advice without compassion to food with no flavor?
- Why are we so quick to give advice to someone who is hurting?
- When we're hurting, why do we get tired of other people's advice?
- Read Job 6:6-7. Why didn't Job's friends speak to him?
- When has a friend shown compassion to you? When have you shown compassion to a friend?
- How does God show us compassion?

Bomb Shelter

TOPIC: *Forgiveness*
SCRIPTURE: *1 Corinthians 6:9-11*
SUPPLIES: *photocopy of the "Character Descriptions" handout (p. 19)*

Before the game, photocopy the "Character Descriptions" handout (p. 19), and cut apart the descriptions.

Give each person a character description. Explain to the players that they're going to pretend the world is on the verge of nuclear war. Fortunately, they have a bomb shelter that can hold half the group. As a group, they must decide who gets to go in the bomb shelter. As individuals, their goal is to get themselves in the bomb shelter, but also to choose other people. Give the group several minutes to talk about their decisions.

If you have more than eighteen people, you'll need more than one copy of the handout, and players will need to form teams to

CHARACTER DESCRIPTIONS

Photocopy and cut out the descriptions. If you have more than eighteen people, make more than one copy. If you have fewer than eighteen, choose the descriptions you like the best (but be sure to include a balance of positive and negative descriptions). *If a description is too sensitive or hits too close to home for some of the participants, don't use it!*

**You're an overachieving high school student.
You succeed in everything you do.**

You're a high school student with a GPA of 1.7.

You're a famous artist.

**You're a criminal. You were convicted of murder,
but you've changed dramatically since being in prison.**

You're an author.

You're a gang leader.

You're a politician.

You're a musician.

You're a mom of three kids and president of the PTA.

You're a high school teacher.

You're a single dad of two kids.

You're a prisoner, and you plan to commit more crimes when you get out.

You're a prostitute.

You're an atheist.

You're a promiscuous teenager.

You're a thief.

You're an alcoholic.

You're a successful businessperson who secretly steals from your company.

---

play. Adjust the number of character descriptions you hand out to match the number of people on each team.

DISCUSSION
• Who did you decide to put in the bomb shelter? Why?
• What was it like to try to convince the group that you should go in the shelter?
• What made this game easy or difficult?
• Read 1 Corinthians 6:9-11. Who is "wicked" in God's eyes?
• Who inherits the kingdom of heaven? How?
• Would God have decided to save the same people you decided to save? Explain.
• How does this game relate to God's forgiveness?

Bound Together

TOPIC: *Parents*

SCRIPTURE: *Colossians 3:12-17, 20*

SUPPLIES: *1 ball of yarn per person (include a variety of colors), scissors*

Have youth form groups of three. Give each group a pair of scissors and three balls of yarn in three different colors. Instruct each group to appoint one person as the "binder." That person will tie the other two team members together as quickly as possible.

The pair of youth to be tied together should stand back to back. The binder must tie the pair at their ankles, knees, hips, hands, and heads. At each point, the binder must use all three colors of yarn. The first group to be successfully tied at all five spots wins.

DISCUSSION

- How was this game similar to your relationship with your parents?
- How can trusting our parents' advice be an example of patience and faith?
- When we obey our parents and honor their decisions, how are we showing evidence of God's Spirit in our lives?
- When our parents are wrong, how does God want us to respond to them?
- How can we thank God for our parents' decisions even when we don't agree?

Building a House of Cards

TOPIC: *Hope*
SCRIPTURE: *Psalm 62:5-6*
SUPPLIES: *1 deck of cards per group of 5 to 7*

Have youth form groups of five to seven people. Give each group a deck of cards, and tell participants that they have ten minutes to build houses with their cards. At the end of ten minutes, have all the students tour the room and (carefully) look at the other students' houses to compare the designs.

DISCUSSION

- Is your house pretty stable and secure? Could it survive a fan blowing on it?
- Is your life more or less secure than this house of cards? Explain.
- What types of things make you feel secure?
- What types of things shake your security?
- Read Psalm 62:5-6. What does it mean to put our hope in the Lord?
- How can putting our hope in the Lord make life easier and more stable?

Bulging Bags

TOPIC: *Popularity*

SCRIPTURE: *1 Samuel 16:7; Luke 7:29-35*

SUPPLIES: *chairs, 1 bag of large balloons for each team, 1 small to medium trash bag per team*

Have youth form at least two teams, with no more than twelve people on a team. There can be as few as two on a team. Give each team a bag of large balloons, and instruct teams to line up as for a relay. Place a chair with a trash bag draped over its back about three feet in front of each team.

To play the game, the first person on each team blows up a balloon as full as possible without popping it, ties it shut, runs to the chair, and stuffs the balloon in the bag. As soon as the first person has tied his or her balloon, the next person in line begins blowing up a balloon.

Play continues until the leader calls time or a team has blown up all its balloons. If your group is small with only a few on a team, call time after three to five minutes. If the group is larger, allow teams to play until one team runs out of balloons. Tell players that the team who runs out first doesn't necessarily win. Winning will depend on how full the balloons are.

The team who fits the most fully inflated balloons in its bag, causing it to be the fattest, wins. The leader is the judge. Just for fun, see which team can pop its bag of balloons the fastest.

DISCUSSION

- Read Luke 7:29-35. How were the Pharisees like the "in crowd" of today?
- Why did Jesus not fit in with the Pharisees?
- How do teenagers struggle to fit in with their peers?
- What kind of pressure does "fitting in" put on people?
- What does it take to fit in with God?

Business of Friendship

TOPIC: *Friendship*

SCRIPTURE: *1 Samuel 18:1-4*

SUPPLIES: *small pieces of heavy card stock (the size of business cards), pencils or pens, basket, 1 piece of notebook paper*

Give each person a blank piece of card stock and a pencil or pen. Instruct teenagers to create business cards for their own imaginary companies. They should not put their own names on the cards. Tell them their company names should define what kinds of friends they are. For example, a good listener might create a card for a business called "Listening Ear Café."

After everyone has created a card, collect all the cards. As you do so, write on a piece of notebook paper each person's name and the company name that person chose. Put all the cards in a basket.

To play the game, give one person the basket of cards. Have everyone else stand in a line. Give the person with the basket one minute to distribute the cards to the people he or she thinks they belong to. Tell youth not to reveal whether they've been given the correct cards.

When all the cards have been handed out, have everyone read aloud the cards they've been given. Check your list to see how many people received the correct cards. Give the person with the basket a score based on the number of right answers.

Have players put the cards back in the basket, and give the basket to another person. Have that person distribute the cards. Keep playing until someone gets them all right or everyone has had a chance to match people with company names.

DISCUSSION

• Which company names best described what a good friend is? Why?
• What characteristics are important for good friends?
• How can each of us work to be a better friend?
• If we actually got paid by a company to be good friends, what things would cause us to get fired?

Button Shuffle

TOPIC: *Forgiveness*

SCRIPTURE: *Luke 17:3-4*

SUPPLIES: *assortment of colored buttons, small box, paper, pens or pencils, table*

Before the game, decide on five color combinations of four to six buttons. Colors may be repeated within a grouping. Write these five combinations on the side of the box that will be nearest your body, circling the one button that will be removed from each combination.

Give each person paper and a pen or pencil. Have youth number their papers 1 through 5. Place the first grouping of buttons on a table for the group to look at for approximately three to five seconds. Don't allow players to write anything down. Cover the buttons with the box. Tilt the box so you can remove the button you selected to remove—careful not to let anyone see the button. *Note: You may need to shield the written color combinations with your body as you remove the button.*

Lift the box, and ask everyone to write down the color of the button that was removed. Repeat the process for each of four remaining groupings of buttons. Then let youth "grade" themselves as you call out the missing button colors for all five rounds.

DISCUSSION

- What kinds of feelings do you have when someone wrongs you?
- If those feelings were colors, what colors would they be?
- If those feelings were color-coded and laid out on a table like these buttons, what buttons would be removed when you forgave someone for the wrong?
- Which "buttons" do you have a tendency to want to hold on to when trying to forgive someone?
- What can you do to remove these "buttons" from your heart so your forgiveness is complete like God's forgiveness of you?

Can I Quote You?

TOPIC: *The Future*

SCRIPTURE: *Romans 8:28-39*

SUPPLIES: *several books and calendars containing quotations, Bibles, slips of paper, pens or pencils, bowl*

I nstruct each person to use the books, calendars, and Bibles to select a quotation to incorporate into his or her planning for the future. Once everyone has chosen a quotation, have youth write their quotations on slips of paper. Place all the slips in a bowl.

One at a time, have participants draw a slip from the bowl and read the quotation aloud to the group. Each person must try to guess who chose the quotation on the slip he or she picked from the bowl. If the guess is incorrect, allow the rest of the group to guess. If no one can guess, the person who chose the quotation should reveal his or her identity.

Repeat the drawing and guessing until all the quotations have been selected, read, and matched with the appropriate people.

DISCUSSION

• What kinds of things did you look for when selecting a quotation?
• How does the quotation you picked affect the way you face the future?
• How can the wisdom of others help you reach your goals?
• How can God's Word help us face the uncertainties of the future?

Candle Capers

TOPIC: *Relationships*

SCRIPTURE: *John 15:1-17*

SUPPLIES: *blindfolds, candles, matches, matchboxes, table, stopwatch*

B efore this game, set up a table at one end of the playing area.
Have youth form groups of any size. Each group should designate one person to be the guide person.

Have each group stand in a straight line, with group members close to one another and facing alternating directions. For example,

Person A faces the front of the room, Person B faces the back of the room, Person C faces the front of the room, and so on. Blindfold everyone in the group except the guide person. The last person in line should be standing next to the table you set up beforehand. Place a candle and a matchbox on the table for each group.

Give the guide person on each team a match. When you say "go," the guide person should hand the match to the next person in line. The team member holding the match passes it to the next person without moving his or her feet. Then that person passes the match on to the next person without moving his or her feet. The group continues passing the match until it reaches the last person in line. As soon as this team member gets the match, he or she takes off the blindfold, lights the match, and quickly lights the candle on the table.

Once the candle is lighted, the guide person on the team tells the team to sit down on the floor. Time the students and then repeat the game, challenging the teams to try to improve their times.

DISCUSSION

• Just as the guide person helped us in this game, how does God help us be discerning in our relationships?
• Read John 15:1-17. How does Jesus' example of a vine describe his relationship with us?
• In what ways does being close to Jesus help us make wise decisions in our relationships?
• How do we sometimes shut our eyes to Jesus' guidance in our relationships with others?

Chain Gang

TOPIC: *Unity*
SCRIPTURE: *Psalm 133:1-3*
SUPPLIES: *none*

Create at least two teams with four or more people. Explain that each team will have three minutes to create the longest "chain" that can be lifted by its ends without breaking. Instruct teams to use any items on their bodies and/or items in the room, and to connect them in any way they can think of. For example, they can remove jewelry, belts, socks, shoestrings, and other items and tie them together. When time is called, the chains should be measured for length and tested for durability. The team with the longest chain that doesn't break when lifted wins.

DISCUSSION

• What made your chain strong or weak?
• Why were some "links" of your chain stronger than others?
• How is a weak link like someone who causes disunity?
• How is a long, connected chain like a unified youth group?

Cheese Spread

TOPIC: *God's Love*
SCRIPTURE: *1 John 4:7-21*
SUPPLIES: *cans of spray cheese spread*

Have youth form teams of seven to fifteen. Place a blob of cheese spread on the nose of one participant on each team. Tell youth that when you give the signal, they'll race to spread cheese to the noses of all their teammates. The first team finished will win.

DISCUSSION

- How is the cheese in this game like God's love?
- How does God want us to respond to his love?
- Read 1 John 4:7-21. According to these verses, what is the proof of a God-filled life?
- In what ways are you different or changed as a result of God's love for you?
- How can we grow to love others more?
- What are some ways you can show God's love among your peers?
- How can our demonstration of love show others what our faith is about?

Circle of Friends

TOPIC: *Differences*

SCRIPTURE: *Romans 14:1; 1 John 4:20-21*

SUPPLIES: *masking tape or chalk*

Have youth form two teams. Have one team stand in the middle of the room and bunch up together as close as possible. Make a circle on the floor with the masking tape or chalk, about twelve inches wider than the group itself. Have the other team stand outside the circle.

When you say "go," the team on the outside should try to pull the members of the team on the inside out of the circle. They can do anything except step inside the circle or hurt someone. Those on the inside may do anything to stay where they are, except hurt someone. After the first round, have the teams switch places and play again.

After both teams have tried being on the inside and the outside of the circle, explain that the next phase is to get everyone inside the circle. They may do this by any means—such as stacking on top of each other or one person lying across the arms of others. All persons on both teams must be completely inside the circle.

DISCUSSION

- Which was more fun—trying to get people outside the circle or trying to get everyone inside? Why?

- Why does our society tend to break people into groups and exclude others?
- What does it take to break into the cliques in your school? What does it take to be pushed out?
- How can we celebrate people's differences rather than alienate others?

Clay People

TOPIC: *God's Power*
SCRIPTURE: *2 Corinthians 4:7-10*
SUPPLIES: *2 different colors of clay or modeling dough (about 1 cup per person), foam ball per 10 people, tarp if your playing area is carpeted*

Before the game, lay a tarp in your playing area if it is carpeted. Have youth form two teams. Give everyone about a cup of clay or modeling dough, one color to each team. Have people create small images of themselves. Each clay person should be about six to eight inches high.

Have players stand their clay people randomly around the room or on the tarp you've laid down, at least four feet apart. Each person should stand next to his or her clay person and guard it. Throw out at least one foam ball.

Players should throw the foam ball at the other team's clay people while they protect their own. Each person must keep one foot stationary during the game. Clay people are out of the game if they get squashed, broken, or knocked over.

During the game, go after stray balls, and throw them back into play.

The color of the last remaining clay person reveals the winning team.

DISCUSSION
- Read 2 Corinthians 4:7-10. What does this Scripture say about clay?
- How are people in real life similar to or different from the clay people in our game?
- What does 2 Corinthians 4:7-10 say about God's power?

• If our game were an analogy for real life, what part would the foam balls play? What part would you play?
• How can we have more of God's power in our lives?

Clothespin Giveaway

TOPIC : *Generosity*
SCRIPTURE : *Malachi 3:10; Luke 6:38; 2 Corinthians 9:6-8; 1 John 3:16-17*
SUPPLIES : *6 to 8 spring clothespins per person*

Give each person six to eight clothespins. Ask participants to attach the clothespins to their clothing. Instruct players that when you begin the game, they should try to give away all their clothespins by attaching them to other people's clothing. The goal is to give away all the clothespins without receiving any from other players.

Stop the trading after several minutes by blowing a whistle or calling the group to order. The winner is the person with the fewest clothespins.

DISCUSSION

• How was this game similar to the way God gives us gifts?
• What are some ways we can give without calling attention to ourselves?
• Why do you think God commands us to give to others?
• How does giving help us grow spiritually?
• What are some inappropriate attitudes we shouldn't have toward giving?
• What are some appropriate attitudes we should have toward giving?

Communication Explanation

TOPIC: *Parents*
SCRIPTURE: *James 1:19*
SUPPLIES: *index cards, pens or pencils*

I nvite parents to attend this meeting and participate in this game. Explain that you'll be playing a parent/teen version of *The Newlywed Game*. After sending the parents to a secluded room, give each teenager an index card and a pen or pencil. Instruct players to record on their cards the answers to the following questions *in the way they think their parent(s) would respond*:

1. The item that caused the most stress in my life this week was (a) my teenager, (b) money, (c) my job.

2. I worry most about my teenager (a) taking drugs, (b) not getting good grades, (c) getting married too early.

3. The thing I like most about my teenager is…

4. The thing that frustrates me most about my teenager is…

5. I am usually right about:…

6. I am usually wrong about…

7. I think what my teenager wants most from me is…

8. If I had a free evening, I would (a) watch TV, (b) go on a date with my spouse, (c) conduct a family meeting, (d) do housework or other house projects.

9. I think my teenager uses money (a) wisely, (b) unwisely, (c) better than I did when I was a teenager.

10. If I could give my teenager one thing, I would give…

After teenagers have recorded their answers, bring the parents back into the room, and have them sit with their teenagers. If some teenagers are without parents, have other parents "adopt" them, or hook them up with youth workers, and encourage them to discuss the questions with their parent(s) at home.

Read the questions aloud one at a time, pausing after each one so the parents can respond and the teenagers can determine if their answers were correct. After each question, have volunteer families share their responses with the rest of the group.

DISCUSSION

• Teenagers, what was it like to answer from your parents' perspective?
• What surprised you about your parents' or your teenagers' answers? Why?
• What did this game reveal about the level of communication in your family?
• Why is it hard to be "quick to listen" and "slow to speak"? How would following this admonition change your relationship with your family?

Crossing the Canyon

TOPIC: *Grace*
SCRIPTURE: *2 Corinthians 12:9*
SUPPLIES: *masking tape or chalk*

Before the game, use masking tape or chalk to mark a starting line and a finish line about thirty feet apart. The space between the lines will represent the canyon.

Have youth form at least two teams, with equal numbers of boys on the teams. The object of the game is for the girls on each team to carry the boys across the canyon. The boys cannot offer any help; they must act completely helpless. Each girl can cross the canyon only once.

It works best if some girls pair up to carry boys across the canyon. A few girls will have to carry boys by themselves since they can cross the canyon only once. Each team will have to figure out the sequence in which they'll cross so everyone can be carried without too much difficulty. The team that finishes first wins.

DISCUSSION

- How did it feel to depend on someone else to get you across the canyon?
- What was it like to carry someone else across the canyon?
- How were the girls in this game like Jesus?
- What is grace?
- What does grace have to do with salvation?

Crystal Clear

TOPIC: *Love*

SCRIPTURE: *John 13:35*

SUPPLIES: *paper, pens or pencils*

Have youth form at least two teams of two to six people. Give each team several pieces of paper and pens or pencils. Instruct each team to choose one person to draw first.

Explain that all teams will be given the same item to draw, but the people drawing won't know what the item is and won't be allowed to speak. The teammates must give instructions on how to draw the item without revealing what it is. In other words, they may describe shapes but not objects. For example, if the item is "house," the teammates might instruct the drawer to draw a square with a triangle sitting on top, then two smaller squares inside and in the top half of the large square, and so on.

Have the team drawers leave the room while you announce an item from the list in the margin to the remaining players (or use an idea of your own). Let drawers return to the room, and explain that each team will have one minute to instruct the drawer. Say, "go!" After one minute, call time and decide who wins a point based on which drawer can identify the picture and/or which team's picture is the clearest.

Have each team choose a new person to be the drawer for the next round. Continue playing until each team member has had a chance to draw and a winning team has been determined.

USE THE FOLLOWING IDEAS FOR THIS GAME, OR USE YOUR OWN IDEAS.

• happy face
• camera
• school bus
• picket fence
• canopy bed
• big-screen TV
• bicycle
• church
• apple tree
• sailboat

DISCUSSION

• What was it like to be the drawer in this game?
• What was it like to give the instructions?
• How is giving good instructions to your drawer similar to loving people to prove we're Christians?
• How clear is the picture the world has of Christianity? Why?

Cut That Out!

TOPIC: *Love*

SCRIPTURE: *John 14:15-24*

SUPPLIES: *13x9-inch pan of rice cereal treats for each group of 5 or 6, plastic knives, paper, pens or pencils*

Have youth form teams of five or six, and give each team a pan of rice cereal treats, paper, and a pen or pencil. Give each person a plastic knife. Tell teenagers that when you say "go," each person should use the plastic knife to cut out a rice cereal treat in the shape of the first letter of his or her name. For example, Kim would cut out the letter "K" and Jack the letter "J."

When all team members have cut out their letters and removed them from the pan, the team must come up with a phrase, rhyme, or funny expression using their letters as the first letters in the words of their phrase. Have each team share its phrase and then invite everyone to eat their rice cereal treats.

DISCUSSION

• We're all known by our names on earth. How does Jesus say he'll know us?
• In what ways does Jesus distinguish between those who love him and those who don't?
• Why does Jesus say that if we love him, we'll obey his commands?

Don't Drop the Ball!

TOPIC: *Maturity*

SCRIPTURE: *1 Peter 2:1-3*

SUPPLIES: *objects that can be easily manipulated, such as balls, chairs, coins, pencils, combs, and drinking or eating utensils*

Have youth form groups of five or six. Instruct each group to select one object from the collection you've provided. Tell participants that each group will create a pantomime of how a certain age level would use the object they have chosen.

Secretly tell each group which age level they'll represent: toddlers, eight-year-olds, teenagers, thirty-somethings, or senior citizens. If you have more than five groups, it's OK to assign more than one group to an age level.

Each group should give a brief one-minute performance of its pantomime. Following the performance, other groups should try to guess the age level the performers were representing.

DISCUSSION

• Why do you think people of different ages use the same objects so differently?
• How does maturity affect the ways we use a given object, such as a ball or chair?
• How do you think our maturity as Christians affects the ways we interpret God's Word?
• How can the process of maturity reveal new uses and "interpretations" of God's Word for you?
• What's a Scripture passage or Bible story that meant one thing to you as a child but has taken on different or greater meaning for your life now?

Easy Skeet Shoot

TOPIC: *Violence*
SCRIPTURE: *Matthew 5:21-22*
SUPPLIES: *paper plates, rubber bands*

Have students form pairs. Give each pair several paper plates and several rubber bands. Explain to pairs that you're giving them two minutes to shoot their paper plates as many times as they can. Instruct partners that they're to work as a team to accomplish this. Partners must remain five steps apart at all times. One person in the pair will toss the paper plates in the air, while the other will shoot rubber bands at the paper plates. After one minute, partners should switch roles.

Have each pair find a place in the room to shoot. When pairs are ready, give them the signal to begin. After one minute, give pairs the signal to switch. After another minute, call time. Congratulate the pair that hit its plates the most often, and congratulate everyone's marksmanship.

DISCUSSION

• Is it OK to pretend to be violent or to pretend to do something violent? Explain.
• What do you consider to be violent? What isn't violent?
• How do you think God feels about violence?
• How should we react to threats of violence? when we see violence?

Fitting In

TOPIC: *Peer Pressure*
SCRIPTURE: *Romans 12:2*
SUPPLIES: *2 large boxes that teenagers can fit in, extra boxes if possible*

Have youth form two teams. Have both teams line up at one end of a large room. Put two large boxes at the other end of the room. Tell participants that when you say "go," the first player on each team must run to that team's box and put as much of his or her body as possible into the box. After the player has fit into the box, he or she will run back and tag the next player. That player will then run down and try to fit in the box. The game continues until everyone on the team has fit in the box. The team that finishes first wins.

In order for a "fit" in the box to count, the box bottom must be flat on the floor. Appoint an adult volunteer as the judge to say whether or not a player has sufficiently fit into the box.

If you have extra boxes available, replace boxes if teenagers break them when trying to fit in.

DISCUSSION

• What are some of the "boxes" you're expected to fit into in our culture?

- When have you tried to "fit in" someplace that was a painful fit? What happened?
- In what ways do people change themselves just to be accepted?
- Why do we put such importance on being accepted by others?
- What happens to people who don't "fit in"?

Flavor of Worship

TOPIC: *Worship*
SCRIPTURE: *Isaiah 29:13-14*
SUPPLIES: *a roll of multicolored LifeSavers candy for each team of 7 to 8*

JUMPSTARTERS

Have teenagers form teams of seven to eight. Have each team line up at one end of the room. Each team should choose one person to be the candy distributor. Give each distributor a roll of LifeSavers candy, and have that person stand at the other end of the room, across from the rest of the team.

On "go," the first person in line should run to the distributor and get a piece of candy. The runner should go back to the line and, without allowing the next person in line (the "flavor taster") to see the color of the candy, place it in that person's mouth. As soon as the flavor taster can tell what flavor the candy is, he or she should whisper the flavor to the runner, who returns to the distributor and whispers the flavor guessed.

If the guess is right, the runner goes to the end of the line, the flavor taster becomes the next runner, and the race is repeated. If the guess is incorrect, the runner returns to the flavor taster and asks for another guess. They must continue until they get it right.

Teams must repeat the process until everyone on the team has had the chance to be a runner.

DISCUSSION

- What are some of the "flavors" of worship that you have seen at other churches?
- What is the purpose of worship?

- How is a roll of LifeSavers candy a lot like worship?
- If you could create the perfect flavor of worship, what would it be?
- How would God be honored by your flavor of worship?

Foot Race

TOPIC: *Servanthood*
SCRIPTURE: *Luke 22:24-27; John 13:12-15*
SUPPLIES: *none*

Ask all participants to remove their socks and shoes and place them in a heap in the center of the room. Then have the group form two teams.

Tell participants that when you say "go," each team should race to put the socks and shoes back on each of its members. No one may retrieve or put on his or her own socks and shoes—someone else must find the shoes and socks and put them on a person's feet. In the meantime, that person will work at putting socks and shoes on the feet of others.

DISCUSSION

- Read John 13:12-15 aloud, followed by Luke 22:24-27. Why did Jesus trouble himself with something the disciples were capable of doing for themselves?
- What did Jesus hope to teach his disciples by washing their feet?
- Why is it sometimes awkward to allow someone else to serve you?
- Who are some people in your life who exemplify servanthood? Explain.
- Why are we sometimes hesitant when we see a service opportunity?
- How can our service efforts show others what God is like?
- What can we do as a group to be better servants?

Friendship Traits

TOPIC: *Friendship*

SCRIPTURE: *Ruth 1:11–2:3*

SUPPLIES: *none*

Have participants form a circle. Have one person begin the game by saying, "I'm going to Judah, and I need a friend who is…" The person should complete the sentence with a character trait of a good friend, such as "trustworthy."

The next person in the circle should say, "I'm going to Judah, and I need a friend who is [trustworthy] and…" The person should finish the sentence with another character trait of a good friend.

Have players continue around the circle in this manner, each person listing all the named traits in order and adding another trait. Continue until everyone in the circle has had a turn.

DISCUSSION

• Which of the traits mentioned in the game are most important in a friend? Why?
• Which of the character traits mentioned do you have to offer a friend?
• Read Ruth 1:11–2:3. How was Ruth a good friend to Naomi?
• How did Ruth demonstrate the character traits we listed in the game?

Future Stories

TOPIC: *The Future*

SCRIPTURE: *Jeremiah 29:11*

SUPPLIES: *3 containers labeled "names," "locations," and "occupations"; 3 slips of paper per person; pens or pencils*

Give each person three slips of paper and a pen or pencil. Have each person write his or her name on one slip of paper. Collect those paper slips, and put them in the container labeled "names." Next, have everyone write down a location, such as a cave, a trash can, or a desert. Encourage creativity. Collect these paper slips, and put them in the container labeled "locations." Finally, have everyone record an occupation, such as homemaker, famous chef, or dogcatcher. Again, encourage creativity. Place these slips in the container labeled "occupations." Mix up the slips in each container.

Have everyone sit in a circle. Explain that participants will take turns telling silly stories about each other's lives in the future. Have teenagers pass the containers around the circle and draw from them so each person has one slip from each of the three containers. Make sure no one gets his or her own name.

Going around the circle, have each person read the three slips of paper together to tell a funny story about someone's life in the future. For example, someone might say, "Jill will grow up, live in a trash can, and be a dogcatcher." Continue until everyone's story has been told.

DISCUSSION

- How would you feel if your future were being determined as randomly as it was in this game? Why?
- If you could have your future foretold, would you? Why or why not?
- What, if any, danger would there be in knowing the future?
- How do you feel knowing that God knows your future?
- How can we learn to trust God more with the future?

Getting It in Focus

TOPIC: *The Bible*
SCRIPTURE: *2 Timothy 2:15*
SUPPLIES: *slides, slide projector, screen*

Before the meeting, fill the slide projector with slides that will be identifiable to your group. The best slides would be pictures of people in your group. Set up a screen so the slides will be easy to see. Be sure your slide projector can easily be brought in and out of focus. If possible, set it up so the first slide will be severely out of focus to begin.

Have teenagers form two teams. Explain that they'll be participating in a contest to see which team can identify the most pictures or faces correctly and quickly. Tell teams to yell out an answer when they know it.

Display the first slide, severely out of focus. Then, as the kids begin to throw out guesses, slowly bring the photo into focus until one team identifies it. Continue the contest until participants have seen and identified all the slides.

DISCUSSION

• Why is it sometimes difficult to identify how the Bible relates to our lives?

• How do we know which Scriptures apply to our lives?

• How can we become more skilled at focusing on Scripture?

Group Barter

TOPIC : *Money/Materialism*

SCRIPTURE : *Ecclesiastes 5:10-11*

SUPPLIES : *photocopies of "Team One Point Values" and "Team Two Point Values" boxes (p. 43); several sheets of white, blue, pink, and yellow paper; scissors*

Before the game, photocopy the "Team One Point Values" and "Team Two Point Values" boxes on page 43. You'll need one copy for each person. Cut each sheet of white, blue, pink, and yellow paper into small strips. The amount of paper you need depends on the number of students you have (see below).

Have participants form two teams. Give each member of Team One the following slips of paper: one pink slip, twenty white slips, ten yellow slips, and two blue slips. Give each member of Team Two the following slips of paper: one blue slip, twenty yellow slips, ten white slips, and two pink slips. Give each person on each team a copy of the appropriate point-value box.

Explain to teams that they'll spend the next few minutes bartering with one another to get as many of the highest value papers for their teams as possible. When you call time, the team with the most points from the slips of paper is the winning team.

Give groups about five minutes to see how many points they can gain. Congratulate everyone's accomplishment.

DISCUSSION

- How is this game like the way we pursue money and material possessions?
- Is it OK to have a lot of money or material possessions? Explain.
- When does the pursuit of money and material possessions become harmful?
- How can pursuit of money and material possessions destroy our relationship with God?

Guiding Light

TOPIC : *Relationships*

SCRIPTURE : *Matthew 5:43-48*

SUPPLIES : *sidewalk chalk, flashlights*

This game should be played at night in a large, dark (but secure!) parking lot.

Before the meeting, use sidewalk chalk to write the following seven words on the pavement in various sections of the parking lot: "love," "hate," "neighbor," "children," "God," "enemies," and "reward." Spread the words out so youth will have to search for them with flashlights.

Have teenagers form groups of three to four people. Give each group a flashlight. Challenge the groups to find as many words on the pavement as possible in three minutes. Allow three minutes for groups to return to the starting point.

DISCUSSION

• What words did you discover in your search?
• What does each of these words tell us about relationships with others?
• What are some of the reasons human relationships can be so difficult?
• What guidelines does Jesus offer us regarding relationships with others?
• How do Jesus' teachings provide light and direction regarding our response to those who hate us?
• What might be the key word Jesus would teach us about relating to others?

Hands Down

TOPIC : *Media*

SCRIPTURE : *Colossians 3:1-17*

SUPPLIES : *list of current popular movies, magazines for teenagers, secular music groups, clothing styles, hairstyles, and jewelry fads*

Have youth form groups of four or five. Instruct group members to sit in a circle on the floor with their legs crossed. Group members should sit close enough so everyone can slap the hands of the people on either side.

Explain that you'll be reading the names of current movies, music groups, and fads aloud. Participants should listen to what you say, then quickly decide if it refers to something Christ would want us to emulate in words, lifestyle, or action. Each time you call out something, youth must be ready to give a hands-up or a hands-down vote to the item in question.

As soon as each group comes to a unanimous decision and can make a convincing case for support or opposition, they should go around their group's circle and either slap each other's hands facing up in support, or slap each other's hands facing down in opposition. The first group to slap hands around the circle gets to share its opinion. Then the other groups can decide whether they agree by giving a hands-up or hands-down vote to their statements. Continue the game until you've completed the list you composed.

DISCUSSION

• What are some ways we can use the Bible as a guide for determining which movies to see, which groups to listen to, and which fads to follow?
• Why does it matter what choices we make when it comes to media?
• How do our entertainment choices and our personal style affect our relationships with God and others?
• How can our media choices affect the way others see God?

Hard-Boiled Egg Toss

TOPIC: *Grace*
SCRIPTURE: *Hebrews 4:16*
SUPPLIES: *1 raw egg and 1 hard-boiled egg with shell intact per 2 people, masking tape*

This game should be played outside or on a noncarpeted floor in a large room. Before the meeting, use masking tape to mark lines on the floor at five-foot intervals across the room. If you're playing outside, use sticks or rocks to mark the intervals.

Have teenagers form pairs, give each pair a raw egg, and explain that pairs will compete in an egg-toss competition. Explain that, beginning five feet away from each other, partners toss the egg to each other and attempt to catch it without breaking it. After each successful egg toss, one partner will move back five feet, while the other will remain in the same place. If a pair drops an egg, that pair is out of the competition. The pair who completes a successful egg toss from the farthest away wins.

After a winner is declared, give each pair a hard-boiled egg, and play the game again.

DISCUSSION

• Why was it easier to catch the hard-boiled egg?
• How did you feel when it was your turn to catch the raw egg?
• What is God's grace?
• How would you feel trying to talk to God without God's grace?
• How is the hard-boiled egg like the freedom God's grace gives us?

Heart of Ice

TOPIC: *Dating*
SCRIPTURE: *2 Timothy 2:22*
SUPPLIES: *ice cubes*

Have teenagers form groups of four or five people. Explain that you'll be distributing something in a few moments and the first group to make it disappear wins. The only restriction on making it disappear is that it cannot be eaten.

Have each group sit in a circle. Give each group an ice cube. Tell teenagers to hold the ice cubes in their hands, rub them between their toes, and keep passing them around the small group until the cube has completely melted and disappeared. Challenge students to work together to melt the ice as fast as possible.

DISCUSSION

• Just as our ice cubes changed, how do we sometimes change when we begin dating someone?
• What are some ways we can safeguard ourselves against temptations in dating?
• What kinds of qualities should we look for in prospective dates?
• What's the best way to decide if you should be in a relationship with someone?
• How can people keep from changing to please dating partners?

Highly Motivated

TOPIC: *School*
SCRIPTURE: *Proverbs 3:5-6*
SUPPLIES: *uninflated balloons, rubber bands*

Note: This game requires a large playing area.

Set out uninflated balloons. Allow participants to take as many balloons as they wish. Then give each participant one rubber band for every balloon he or she took. Instruct students to inflate their balloons and tie off each one with a rubber band.

When all the balloons have been inflated and tied off, tell participants that the object of the game is to keep all the balloons up in the air at the same time for as long as possible. Once a balloon touches the floor, its owner is "out" and should be seated.

DISCUSSION

• What made this game more difficult for some people than for others?
• How does this game compare to the ways individual people deal with pressure in school?
• Why do some people face more pressure in school than others do?

- How can your relationship with God help you deal with the pressures of school?
- How can your relationship with God motivate you to succeed in school?

How to Make a Peanut Butter and Jelly Sandwich

TOPIC: *Dating*

SCRIPTURE: *Song of Songs 8:4*

SUPPLIES: *bread, knives, peanut butter, jelly, paper plates, table, chairs*

J
U
M
P
S
T
A
R
T
E
R
S

Before this game, set out bread, knives, peanut butter, jelly, and paper plates on a table.

Have teenagers form pairs. Explain to the group that the pairs are going to compete in a contest to see who can make the best peanut butter and jelly sandwich. The catch is that one person is going to give the instructions without looking at his or her partner, who must follow the instructions. The person following the instructions must pretend that he or she has never made a sandwich and must rely only on the partner's advice. For example, if the partner giving instructions says, "First, put the peanut butter on the bread,"

the partner following the instructions might put the jar of peanut butter on top of the unopened loaf of bread.

Have one partner in each pair stand at the table with the sandwich supplies. The other partner should sit on a chair behind the person at the table, facing away from the table. Give pairs several minutes to make their sandwiches. Monitor the contest to be sure sandwich-makers are following their partners' instructions.

When pairs have finished, affirm them for their creativity, accuracy, or other fun sandwich-making characteristics, and invite them to eat their sandwiches.

DISCUSSION

• Partners giving instructions, what made your job easy or difficult?
• Partners receiving instructions, what made your job easy or difficult?
• What would have made this game easier? Why?
• What happens when we don't follow the right procedures in real-life situations?
• Read Song of Songs 8:4. What do you think this verse means?
• Why do you think God cares what we do in dating relationships?
• How can we avoid making bad decisions in dating relationships?

Huddle Hustle

TOPIC: *Family*
SCRIPTURE: *Genesis 45:1-15*
SUPPLIES: *masking tape*

Before the game, use masking tape to mark a starting line and a finish line several feet apart.

Have teenagers form teams of five to ten. Ask each team to stand in a huddle, as close together as possible. Encourage teams to hold on tightly to one another—if a huddle is broken, that team will forfeit. Tell teams to stand behind the starting line until you say go. When you give the signal, huddles should race to the finish line.

DISCUSSION

• How does this game remind you of your family life?

- Read Genesis 45:1-15 aloud. How does this account show the importance Joseph placed on family?
- What things today might test even the strongest family?
- What can a family do to grow closer?
- Why is forgiveness an important part of family life?
- What qualities do you most admire about the people in your family?
- What can you do to show your family members they're important to you?

Human Boggle

TOPIC: *Leadership*
SCRIPTURE: *1 Corinthians 12:14-27*
SUPPLIES: *paper, markers, tape*

Have teenagers form teams of five or six. Each team should designate a leader. The leader will assign all other team members a letter of the alphabet, assigning at least two vowels. Give each team paper, a marker, and tape. Ask each person to write his or her assigned letter on a piece of paper, filling the whole page. Have team members tape their letters to their backs.

When each team has finished preparing, ask each team to stand in a row. When you say "go," the leader of each team should go to work arranging the "letters" into words. When a team has formed a word, record that word on a piece of paper.

Call time after several minutes.

LEADER TIP

Especially if you have a large group, it helps to have other adults help you with this game. Assign each adult to a team or a few teams, and have adults keep track of the words for the team(s) they've been assigned.

DISCUSSION

- What important role did the leader play in this game?
- What are some practical reasons God has called some of us to lead and others to follow?
- Are you more of a leader or a follower?
- What qualities make a person a good leader?
- How can we encourage those who lead us?
- How can we encourage those serving behind the scenes?

Incorrect Labels

TOPIC : *Acceptance*
SCRIPTURE : *Romans 15:5-7*
SUPPLIES : *self-stick labels, poster boards*

Before the game, print the following sentences on self-stick labels, with one word on each label. The order of the words should be mixed up so the phrases can't be easily identified. You'll need one complete set of labels for each team.

- Together everyone achieves more.
- Table the label; accept me for me.
- There's no "I" in "team."
- You're nobody until somebody loves you.

Have teenagers form teams of five to eight. Have each team line up in single file. Give the first person in each line poster board, and give the last person in each line a set of printed labels.

Explain that each set of labels contains four complete sentences when put together correctly. On "go," the last person in each row should begin peeling off one label at a time and sending it to the front of the line. With the help of his or her team, the first person must put each word in the correct spot on the poster board to complete the four sentences. The first team to do so wins. If no team gets all four sentences correct, award points to the team with the most correct.

DISCUSSION

- How do you feel when others don't include you?
- How well do the phrases on these poster boards address the issue of acceptance in real life?
- What does it mean to be a team?
- As Christians, what should we do to be more accepting of others?

Inhale, Exhale

TOPIC: *Grace*
SCRIPTURE: *Romans 5:1-21*
SUPPLIES: *straws, round cereal puffs, empty soda bottles*

J
U
M
P
S
T
A
R
T
E
R
S

Have youth form teams of four to six people. Have teams line up in single file. Give each person a straw and a piece of cereal.

When you say "go," the first person in each line must place the straw between his or her lips and suck on it to pick up the piece of cereal. Each person must walk to the other end of the room with the cereal still stuck to the straw and then drop the cereal into the top of an empty soda bottle.

As soon as one team member successfully walks the length of the room with the cereal on the straw and drops it into the bottle, the next person in line can begin. If the cereal falls on the floor, the player must bend down and suck it up onto the straw without using any hands. Challenge the teams to try to complete the course as quickly as possible.

DISCUSSION

- How was this game like trying to work out problems without God's grace?
- How does God's grace bring us freedom?

- When have you felt the grace of God most vividly?
- How could you describe grace to someone else?
- What do we mean when we say grace is a gift from God?

Instant Artists

TOPIC: *Creation*

SCRIPTURE: *Isaiah 64:8*

SUPPLIES: *modeling dough or clay, a unique object, stopwatch*

Divide students into teams of six, and give each person a handful of modeling dough or clay. Ask the teams to sit in single file lines, with all of the students facing one side of the room. Explain that the one exception is the last person in the line, who must turn around and face the opposite direction. When students are situated, tell them that they cannot speak to their teammates for the next six minutes.

Show all of the last students in each line a unique object (such as a stuffed animal or a figurine), and tell them that they have only one minute to mold their clay into the likeness of the object. Once their minute is up, they need to quickly turn around and pass their models to the people in front of them, who then have only one minute to mold their own lumps of clay to look like their team members' models. When they have finished, have them pass their own sculpture to the students in front of them. Have students continue to pass their clay sculptures in this manner, taking only one minute to create a model that matches the one passed to them by their teammates.

When the six minutes are up, show the entire group the original object, and challenge teams to see how close their final sculptures came to the original model.

DISCUSSION
- How close did the final clay figures come to the actual likeness of the model?
- How is the game we just played similar to how God created the world? How is it different?
- Read Isaiah 64:8. What does this verse mean?

• How do you feel knowing that God created everything that exists?
• What are some of God's creations that you consider to be miraculous?

The Judge Says...

TOPIC: *Mercy*
SCRIPTURE: *James 2:12-13*
SUPPLIES: *none*

Have one volunteer play the part of the Judge for this version of the game Simon Says. The Judge should think of difficult tasks for the rest of the group to perform and give them commands in rapid succession. Before some tasks, the Judge should say, "The Judge says," and before others the Judge should say nothing. Suggestions for tasks include hopping on your left foot four times, turning twice to the right, skipping once, hopping twice, and squatting.

Each time someone performs a task without the Judge saying, "The Judge says," that person is out of the game. If someone fails to complete a required task successfully, that person is also out of the game. The Judge can determine whether someone has satisfactorily completed a task. The Judge should use high, even harsh, standards in this game. Throughout the game, the tasks should become increasingly difficult until everyone is out of the game.

DISCUSSION
• What made this game difficult?
• What was it like to feel no mercy from the judge?
• How would this game have been different if the judge had been merciful?
• How did this game compare to the way God treats us?
• What is God's mercy?
• How can God be just and merciful at the same time?

Just Ask for It

TOPIC: *Wisdom*

SCRIPTURE: *James 1:5*

SUPPLIES: *lyrics or music to 9 different songs*

Before the game, ask an adult or youth volunteer to be your accomplice for this game. Clue that person in on the secret to this game so you can demonstrate how it works. Ask that person to volunteer to go first.

On the floor, lay out lyrics or music to nine different songs as shown in the diagram in the margin. Tell the group that you're going to send a volunteer out of the room. Your group will choose one of the nine songs while the volunteer is gone. When the volunteer comes back into the room, he or she will try to guess which song the group has chosen.

Silent Night	Pass It On	As the Deer
Resurrection	Joy of My Life	Jesus is the Rock
He Touched Me	Have Thine Own Way	White as Snow

Ask your accomplice volunteer to leave the room. While he or she is gone, have the group pick one song from the nine that are laid out on the floor. Then allow the volunteer back in the room.

Tell the volunteer that he or she will have to guess which song the group chose. Then point to any song and ask, "Is it this one?"

When you point to that first song, be sure to point to the area on that paper that indicates the position in the grid of the song the group chose. For example, if the group chose the song in the upper right hand corner of the grid, touch the upper right hand corner of the first piece of sheet music as you ask, "Is it this one?" That will tell your volunteer that the song the group has chosen is the one in the upper right hand corner of the grid of nine songs.

Keep pointing to songs (after the first song you touch, you can point to any part of the paper) and asking, "Is it this one?" Your volunteer should answer "no" until you touch the song the group chose. At that point, your volunteer should know to answer "yes."

Challenge the group to figure out how your volunteer knew which song the group chose. Choose another volunteer, and send that person out of the room. Have the group choose another song. When the volunteer returns, play the game again until he or she guesses the song or gives up.

Continue to play until some teenagers figure it out. If someone thinks he or she has figured it out, have that person be the next volunteer to guess the song. Continue to challenge the group to figure it out until everyone does or gives up.

DISCUSSION

• How did it feel to play this game when you didn't know the solution?
• How was this game different when you did know the solution?
• When does life seem as confusing as this game?
• How can God's wisdom change how we experience life?
• Read James 1:5. What does this Scripture say about God's wisdom?

Kaboom!

TOPIC : *Friendship*
SCRIPTURE : *Ecclesiastes 4:10*
SUPPLIES : *string or strips of fabric, uninflated balloons*

Set out uninflated balloons at one end of the playing area. Have teenagers form pairs, and give each pair string or a strip of fabric. Have partners stand side by side and tie their inside legs together just above the knees. Then have partners lock their inside arms together. The person on the right can use only his or her right arm, and the person on the left can use only his or her left arm. Have everyone stand at the end of the room opposite the balloons.

The object of this game is for each pair to run to the opposite end of the room, pick up a balloon, blow it up, and tie it. Remember, partners can use only their free arms.

Once partners have blown up a balloon and tied it off, they must run back to the starting end of the room, place the balloon on the floor, and sit on it until it pops.

DISCUSSION

- What would this game have been like if you had been using only one of your own hands, without the help of your partner?
- How was this game similar to having friends in real life?
- What are some ways friends help us?
- Why might the kinds of friends we associate with be important?
- What do you look for in a friend? Why?

Leadership Scramble

TOPIC: *Leadership*
SCRIPTURE: *Exodus 3:7-12*
SUPPLIES: *none*

Form even teams of at least four people. Explain that you'll call out instructions on how to determine a group leader, and when the group determines who the leader is, everyone but the leader should quickly sit down. The first group to choose the correct leader and sit down wins the point for that round.

Each round, call out one of the following instructions for groups to use to determine the leader:

- the person who has the longest hair
- the person who has the busiest schedule
- the person who has the shortest last name
- the person who is the shortest
- the person who has the largest feet
- the person who can jump the highest
- You choose your leader!

Teams should try to earn as many points as possible.

DISCUSSION

- How did the instructions in this game compare to the way leaders are determined in real life?
- Does every person have the capability to be a leader? Why or why not?
- What hinders some people from taking on leadership roles?
- Read Exodus 3:7-12. How does God's answer to Moses make you feel about your leadership potential?

Let's Make a Deal

TOPIC: *Body Image*

SCRIPTURE: *Ephesians 2:10*

SUPPLIES: *none*

Have teenagers form teams of eight to ten people (with fairly equal numbers of guys and girls on each team). Tell participants that you're going to award points to each team based on all the different unique items they can come up with from their purses or pockets. On "go," everyone will go through their pockets and purses to bring out as many unique items as they can. They'll get points only for the items no other team has.

Give teams three minutes to compile what they consider unique from their belongings. Award points for all the unique items.

DISCUSSION

- How would someone describe you, based on what is in your purse or pockets?
- How would this description differ from the way you really want to be described?
- How is this similar to the way we feel about our body image?
- How can we begin to feel better about ourselves, regardless of how others see us?

Look Ahead

TOPIC: *The Future*

SCRIPTURE: *Matthew 24:36-47*

SUPPLIES: *newspapers, highlighter markers*

Have teenagers form two teams. Give each team a small stack of newspapers and highlighter markers. Then tell participants that each team has ten minutes to find stories which reflect some belief about the future, such as a story about a doomsday cult, an article about someone who made a prediction for the rise or fall of the stock market, or a column about any future events or beliefs.

LEADER TIP

For a surefire game, mix in a few tabloid magazines.

After ten minutes, see which team has found the most articles. Invite each team to read a couple of the stories it found.

DISCUSSION

• Which of these newspaper stories was the most preposterous? Why?

• Why do you think people have a fascination with the future?

• Read Matthew 24:36-47. What did Jesus say about the future in this Bible passage?

• Why do you think Jesus warned his disciples about predicting the future?

• How might the church today have fallen into the trap of predicting the future?

• What, according to Jesus, is more important than predicting the future?

• What principles might we use to help us when the future seems bleak or hopeless?

Losers Win

TOPIC: *Mercy*
SCRIPTURE: *Matthew 5:7*
SUPPLIES: *2 hats, 2 pairs of gloves, chairs, treats*

Have teenagers form two teams. Line up two rows of chairs facing each other. Set one hat at one end of each team's row of chairs, and place the gloves at the other end. Each team should sit in a row of chairs.

Explain that this game is a sitting relay race. Each team will pass the hat down the row, and it must touch the top of each team member's head before it's passed on. Once the hat has reached the other end, the team will pass the gloves down the row, with each team member putting them on before passing them on. The first team to pass the hat and the gloves down the entire row wins.

After the winning team has been announced, give treats to each person on the *losing* team. Then hand out treats to the winners.

DISCUSSION
- How did you feel when the game was over and I rewarded the losing team?
- What is mercy?
- How did this game demonstrate mercy?
- How can you show mercy in everyday life?
- How does God show mercy toward us?

Media Memory

TOPIC: *Media*
SCRIPTURE: *2 John 1:9-11*
SUPPLIES: *none*

Have students sit in a circle. Explain that they're going to play a memory game based on the media. One person will name a favorite television show, movie, or character played on television or in a movie. Then that person will point to someone else, who must name a character, TV show, or movie that begins with the last letter of the character, TV show, or movie just named. For example, someone might say, "Oprah Winfrey." He or she would then point to another person, who might say, "Yentl."

Continue playing until someone gets stumped, then begin again if you like.

DISCUSSION
- How much impact does the media have on our lives? How can you tell?
- What's the best way to evaluate the images and themes we see in the media?
- What makes some media images so damaging?
- How do you think God feels about what we view on television and at the movies?

Morality Cups

TOPIC: *Peer Pressure*

SCRIPTURE: *1 Corinthians 5:9-11*

SUPPLIES: *4 buckets, water, paper cups*

Note: This game should be played outside or in an area where you don't mind getting water on the floor.

Have teenagers form two teams. Have each team form a line, and have the lines face each other in the center of the playing area. Place a bucket of water at one end of each line, and an empty bucket at the other end of each line.

Explain that each team will try to move the water in the full bucket to the empty bucket at the other end of the line. To do so, team members will take turns filling a paper cup with water, carrying it to the other end by walking between the lines, and dumping the water in the empty bucket. As people walk between the lines with their cups of water, the other team can try to spill the water. Encourage them to be gentle, though, making sure no one gets hurt. And tell everyone that he or she must walk—not run—at all times.

Once the person at the front of the line has filled a cup, carried it between the lines, and dumped it in the bucket at the end of the line, that person joins the end of the line. Then the person who is now at the front of the line takes a turn.

Give each person a paper cup, and start the game. Let teenagers play until each team member has had a turn, or call time after several minutes. Determine which team has the most water in the bucket at the end of the line.

DISCUSSION

• What made this game difficult?

• How was this game similar to facing peer pressure in everyday life?

• When have you felt like someone was trying to cause you to violate your standards of right and wrong?

• What makes peer pressure so powerful?

• How can God help us deal with peer pressure?

Musical Hats

TOPIC: *Family*
SCRIPTURE: *1 Timothy 5:1-8*
SUPPLIES: *cassette player or CD player, cassette tape or CD of music, variety of hats (such as a man's dress hat, a farmer's cap, a dressy lady's hat, a child's cap, and a baseball cap)*

B efore the game, collect enough hats for everyone in the group minus one person.

Distribute hats to everyone except one person. Play some music. While the music is playing, the person without a hat should try to take a hat from someone who has one. As soon as someone else is without a hat, that person should try to take a hat from another person. Participants aren't allowed to hold onto their hats with their hands.

After a few moments, stop the music. When the music stops, whoever is without a hat is out of the game. Take one hat out of the game, and start the music again. Continue in this manner until only one hat is left. The last person left with a hat is the winner.

DISCUSSION

- What various "hats" do family members wear in your family?
- In your family, who plays the most different roles? Why?
- How can you work together to make your roles easier?
- How do you honor your parents?
- How can you become a better family member?

Musical Prayers

TOPIC: *Prayer*

SCRIPTURE: *Matthew 6:7-8; 7:7-12*

SUPPLIES: *chairs, music, 1 written prayer per player, CD player or cassette player, CD or cassette of music*

Before this game, set up a circle of chairs. Place a written prayer on each chair.

Tell teenagers that they're going to be playing a variation of musical chairs. Play some music as players walk around the circle of chairs. When the music stops, each person must stop at a chair, pick up the prayer, and quickly read it aloud. Players must read their entire prayers and may sit down only after they've said "amen."

The last player to sit down must leave the circle. Remove the person's chair, and play again until only one player is left.

DISCUSSION

- Why weren't the prayers in this activity very meaningful?
- How is this game similar to the way people sometimes pray in real life?
- Read Matthew 6:7-8; 7:7-12. What did Jesus say in these verses about praying?
- How can we keep our prayers meaningful?

No Jelly

TOPIC: *Acceptance*

SCRIPTURE: *Matthew 7:1-5; John 13:34*

SUPPLIES: *bread, peanut butter, variety of other ingredients (see below), paper, pens or pencils, blindfolds*

Before the game, create a variety of peanut butter sandwiches, all without jelly. You may want to try the following suggestions: peanut butter and bananas, peanut butter and orange marmalade, peanut butter and pickles, peanut butter and marshmallow fluff, peanut butter and golden raisins, peanut butter and mayonnaise, peanut butter and honey, peanut butter and bacon, peanut butter and wheat germ. Eight to ten variations are good for this game. You'll need at least one sandwich per person.

Have teenagers form teams of four to six people, and have each team appoint a recorder (ideally, the person on the team who is squeamish about taste-testing sandwiches). Give each recorder paper and a pen or pencil. Everyone else on the team should be blindfolded.

Explain that teams will taste-test peanut butter sandwiches to guess what they contain besides peanut butter. Each sandwich must be tasted by at least one person on the team. Assure participants that each sandwich is edible.

Give each team a plate of sandwiches. Allow players to sample the sandwiches and guess what they contain. The recorder should write down the team's guesses, along with the correct ingredients.

When teams have tried all their sandwiches and guessed the mystery ingredients, have recorders report how many correct guesses their teams had.

DISCUSSION

- How would you feel if I used this game as a test, accepting people who like the sandwiches I like, and rejecting those who don't?
- How were the sandwiches in this game similar to the standards we use to accept or reject others?
- What are some of the standards we use to judge other people?
- How have you seen people change themselves to try to be accepted by others?

- How have you seen rejection affect people?
- Read Matthew 7:1-5 and John 13:34. Why does God want us to accept people we don't like?

Paper Sack Potential

TOPIC: *Stewardship*

SCRIPTURE: *Matthew 25:14-30*

SUPPLIES: *paper, pens or pencils, paper sacks, empty paper towel or toilet paper tubes, transparent tape, pencils, cotton balls, cotton swabs, gift bows, Matchbox cars or other small toys, spoons, empty soda cans*

Before the game, fill one paper sack for every four or five people, each with the following items: two empty paper towel or toilet paper tubes, a roll of transparent tape, a pencil, three cotton balls, two cotton swabs, a gift bow, a Matchbox car or other small toy, a spoon, and two empty soda cans.

Have teenagers form groups of four or five, and give each group one of the paper sacks you filled beforehand. Have each group choose a secretary, and give each secretary paper and a pen or pencil.

Explain that groups will have ten minutes to come up with as many uses as possible for the items in their paper sacks. The secretaries should record the uses their groups come up with. The uses can be obvious (like holding paper towels) or made-up (like using an empty tube as a funnel to keep drool off your chin when you spit). Groups may combine the items to create additional ideas, like using the empty tube as a tunnel for the car to drive through. Encourage them to be creative—the sky's the limit!

The group with the most uses listed at the end of ten minutes wins. For fun, let each group share from its list of potential uses.

DISCUSSION

- How difficult was it to think of uses for your items? Why?
- What surprised you about some of the ideas people thought of?
- How is creating new uses for ordinary items like being a good steward with the resources God has given us?

- Why do we sometimes fail to use our resources to their full potential?
- How can we become better stewards of what God has given us?

Paper-Wad Ball

TOPIC: *Worship*
SCRIPTURE: *1 Thessalonians 5:16-18*
SUPPLIES: *scrap paper*

Have teenagers form teams of seven to ten people. Ask each team to stand in a circle. Give each team a piece of scrap paper, and ask teams to crumple their papers into balls.

Explain that when you give the signal, each team should toss its paper ball into the air. Team members must try to keep the paper-wad ball in the air as long as possible by batting it upward with their open palms. The team to keep their paper wad in the air longest will win. Repeat several times.

For an extra challenge, add more paper wads so each team is batting around several paper balls.

DISCUSSION

- How is a paper wad in continual motion like the way our worship should be?
- How would you define worship?
- Read 1 Thessalonians 5:16-18 aloud. How do we go about worshipping "continually"?
- What aspects of worship are you good at? What parts need a little work?
- What are some reasons Jesus deserves our whole-hearted worship?
- How can we glorify God by the way we live?

Parent Trap

TOPIC: *Parents*
SCRIPTURE: *Ephesians 6:1-4*
SUPPLIES: *paper, pens or pencils*

Before the game, write down several typical statements parents might make each day—both positive and negative. Here are some suggested statements: "Do your homework," "Be back by eleven," "I'm proud of you," "Tell me the truth," "Keep up the good work," "Where are you going?" "I love you," "What's going on?" "So tell me about this person you're dating," "Clean up your room," and "Need the car?"

Give each person paper and a pen or pencil. Read each of the parents' statements, and invite students to write down a score from 1 to 10 points for each statement to indicate the likelihood of their parents saying that statement (1 = not very likely; 10 = very likely).

After you've read all the statements, invite students to tally their scores to see who has the most "real" parent.

DISCUSSION

• Which of these statements do teenagers most commonly hear from parents?
• What do you think are some of the challenges to parenting today?
• What's the most important thing you'd like your parents to know about yourself?
• Read Ephesians 6:1-4. What principles for parenting do we find in this Bible passage?
• What do you think is the goal of being a good parent?
• How can you help your mom and/or dad to be better parents?

Picture Verses

TOPIC: *The Church*

SCRIPTURE: *Ephesians 4:11-16*

SUPPLIES: *Bibles, old magazines, glue, poster boards, markers*

J
U
M
P
S
T
A
R
T
E
R
S

Have teenagers form groups of five or six. Give each group a Bible, a stack of old magazines, glue, poster board, and a marker.

Instruct each group to look through the magazines to create a word picture that illustrates a verse in the Bible. Groups will have twenty minutes to choose verses and create their word pictures on the poster boards. They can use words between pictures if necessary. For example, a group may create the word picture below to illustrate Psalm 23:2.

When groups have finished creating their word pictures, have them get back together and present their posters while the other groups guess what the verses are.

DISCUSSION

• How did you decide which verse to use?
• How did you work together to create your posters?
• What is the purpose of the church?
• How do Christians work together to make the church function?
• How can we make our church more effective in fulfilling its purpose?

Please Step Forward

TOPIC: *Siblings*
SCRIPTURE: *1 John 2:9-11*
SUPPLIES: *none*

Explain that in this game, someone will have the opportunity to hire a new brother or sister, and everyone is in the running. First ask a volunteer to be the chooser. Have the chooser stand against one wall, facing the wall. Have everyone else stand against the opposite wall facing the chooser.

The chooser should list qualifications like "must be a boy," "must be in tenth grade," or "must be able to drive." As the chooser lists qualifications, those who fulfill the qualifications should take one step forward. The people who don't fulfill a qualification should sit on the floor. The chooser should continue to list qualifications until only one person is left.

Repeat the game several times, using a different chooser each time.

DISCUSSION

• Choosers, were you surprised at who you picked to be your new brothers or sisters? Why or why not?
• How might life be different if we could choose our brothers and sisters?
• Why do you think God gives us brothers and sisters?
• How can we be better brothers and sisters?

Power-Up Olympics

TOPIC: *God's Power*
SCRIPTURE: *Psalm 18:1-3*
SUPPLIES: *none*

Have teenagers form teams of four. Explain that teams will be competing in an Olympic competition. One person on the team must do twenty push-ups, another must do twenty sit-ups, another must do twenty jumping jacks, and the fourth person must skip across the room and back. (If your group isn't divisible by four, join a group or form a couple of teams of three, with one person participating in two events.)

This competition will be done relay style. When one person completes the twenty push-ups, the second person may begin the sit-ups, and so on. The first team to complete all four events wins.

DISCUSSION

• What was difficult about this event? What made it easy?
• What types of strength or power were needed for this event?
• How is physical strength different from spiritual strength?
• In what ways does God give us strength or power each day?
• How does God provide power for living?

Pressure

TOPIC: *Stress*
SCRIPTURE: *Romans 8:38-39; Ephesians 3:14-19*
SUPPLIES: *paper cups, water, tables*

Before the game, set up tables at one end of your playing area. Cover the tables with paper cups filled with water. This game is best played outside. If you play it indoors, be prepared for lots of spilling water.

Have teenagers form at least two teams, with no more than ten people on each team. Have teams line up for a relay at the end of the room away from the tables you set up beforehand. Have an adult volunteer ready with extra cups and water for the inevitable spillage.

On "go," the first person in each line should walk to the other end of the room, bring back one cup of water, and hand it to the second person in line. The second person should carry the cup of water to the other end and grab another cup, bringing back two cups. Person three brings back three cups of water, and so on. Eventually, you'll have students trying to carry eight, nine, or even ten cups of water.

Caution participants to walk—not run—during this game, and to be careful of spilled water. In case of a spill, the team member who is currently "in play" must return to the water table and refill the cups.

Teams should try to get everyone to the table and back as fast as they can.

DISCUSSION

• What are some things in your life that create stress for you?
• How do you handle stress?
• How much of the stress in your life is under your control?
• How can God help you handle stress?

Prodigal Tag

TOPIC: *Family*
SCRIPTURE: *Luke 15:11-32*
SUPPLIES: *1 blindfold per 2 participants*

Have teenagers form pairs. One partner in each pair must wear a blindfold. The other partner should guide the blindfolded person by keeping his or her hands on the blindfolded partner's waist and shouting out directions.

Choose one pair to be "It." The object is for the blindfolded person in the "It" pair to tag another blindfolded person. As soon as someone is tagged, that person's pair becomes "It."

Play for fifteen to twenty minutes or until pairs are exhausted!

DISCUSSION

• How did it feel to be blindfolded in this game?
• How was this game similar to being part of a family?
• What kinds of guidance can we give other members of our families?
• How do we affect our families when we make blind choices or bad decisions?
• What can we do to be better members of our families?

Puzzled

TOPIC: *Dating*
SCRIPTURE: *2 Corinthians 6:14*
SUPPLIES: *4 children's puzzles*

Before the game, remove one piece from each of four children's puzzles. Then replace the missing puzzle piece with a piece from another puzzle so each puzzle has one wrong piece. Put the puzzles on the floor in four separate piles, with the pieces mixed up.

Have teenagers form four teams. Tell teams that they're simply going to assemble a puzzle as fast as they can. After several minutes, teams will realize they each have one wrong puzzle piece. Remind teams that they aren't finished until their puzzles are complete with all the correct pieces. Once all the teams have finished, congratulate the students for their great teamwork.

DISCUSSION

- How did you realize your team had a puzzle piece missing?
- How is looking for a missing puzzle piece similar to dating?
- How does God's will relate to our dating relationships?
- How can we make wise choices when it comes to dating?

Quiz Me

TOPIC: *School*
SCRIPTURE: *Mark 12:30*
SUPPLIES: *paper, pens or pencils*

Have teenagers form two groups. Explain that groups are going to "test" each other. Each group should develop five questions about any topic. Questions need to be answerable (nothing too personal or too specific that nobody has had the opportunity to learn). Encourage them, however, to think of questions that they know a lot about that other people might not.

After groups create their questions, have them take turns asking the other group the questions.

DISCUSSION

• How might the information in this game be useful?
• What is the value of school?
• Read Mark 12:30. What do you think it means to love God with your entire mind?
• How can classes like biology, math, history, chemistry, or literature help us to love God more?
• What can we do to love God more with our minds?

Reach-It Relay

TOPIC: *God's Love*
SCRIPTURE: *Psalm 57:10*
SUPPLIES: *miscellaneous objects to create a simple obstacle course (such as folding chairs, cardboard boxes, and tables), 1 ball of any type per 3 people*

Before the game, set up a simple obstacle course in a wide-open space (preferably outside). For example, include two tables end to end to crawl under, a tree to run around three times, cardboard boxes to step in and out of, and so on. At the end of the course, place enough balls for each team of three to have one.

Have teenagers form teams of three. Have each team line up single file at the beginning of the obstacle course. Explain the obstacle course step by step. Instruct teams to go through the course, pick up a ball, and go back through the course again.

Here's the catch: Team members must complete the course all together, in a single file line, by following two rules. First, two team members must be touching at all times. Second, only the last person in line at any given time can move, and that person must run to the front of the line and touch the first person in line. Once they've touched, the first person must freeze as the last person runs to the front. After everyone understands, shout, "Go!" Challenge teams to complete the course in the correct fashion and arrive back at the beginning with their ball as fast as they can.

DISCUSSION

• What was frustrating about this game?

- How did the limitations of this game make you feel?
- What are the limitations of human love?
- How is trying to reach the ball in this game like trying to reach a non-Christian friend with human love?
- How does it make you feel to know that God's love reaches farther than we can imagine and has no limitations?

Reaching the Heights

TOPIC: *Prayer*

SCRIPTURE: *Psalm 5:1-3*

SUPPLIES: *anything that easily floats on air such as balloons, feathers, tissues, and cotton balls*

Have teenagers form teams of four to six. Give each team an object that easily floats on air. Tell team members that they need to work together to get their object to touch the ceiling. They can't use their hands; they must make the object rise by blowing on it. The first team to make their object touch the ceiling wins. Have teams switch objects and try again.

DISCUSSION

- How are the floating objects in this game similar to how we sometimes feel about prayer?
- Why does it sometimes seem like others' prayers are getting through to God but ours aren't?
- How can asking others to join us in prayer help when we have a prayer concern?

Servant Relay

TOPIC: *Servanthood*
SCRIPTURE: *Matthew 20:26b-28*
SUPPLIES: *2 sets of clothing large enough to be worn by anyone in the group containing the same types of items such as pants, a jacket, a hat, a scarf, and gloves*

Have teenagers form two teams. Teams should line up at one end of the room. At the opposite end, place the two sets of clothing.

Explain that when the relay begins, the first two people from each team will run to the clothing. Person A will dress Person B in the clothing. When Person B is fully clothed, the two people will run back to the team, and Person B will touch the next person in line. The two of them will then run back to the other end of the room. Person B will then take off the clothing and dress the new person.

Teams will continue until everyone has been both the person dressing and the person dressed. Students should work together to finish the relay as quickly as possible.

DISCUSSION

- How did it feel to have someone help you dress? Was it a positive or negative experience? Why?
- What was it like to help someone else dress?
- In real life, is it easier for you to serve or to be served? Why?
- Why do you think God calls us to serve one another?
- How can we become better at serving others as Jesus did?

Service With a Smile

TOPIC: *Servanthood*
SCRIPTURE: *Matthew 7:12*
SUPPLIES: *photocopy of the "Jobs List" handout (p. 77), scissors, hat or box*

Before the game, make a photocopy of the "Jobs List" handout (p. 77), and cut apart the job strips. Place the strips in a hat or box.

To begin the game, allow each teenager to pick a job strip from the hat. Players should take turns acting out the occupations listed on their strips, without saying anything. The rest of the group will try to guess the occupation from the actions.

DISCUSSION

- What types of work do we most commonly associate with helping others?
- How might one be a servant to others in the various occupations we acted out?
- How can we demonstrate what Jesus taught in the work we do each day?
- Why do you think we often consider service to be outside our work environment?
- How might our daily work become a type of service to others?
- How can we incorporate a spirit of servanthood into daily life?

Share Alike

TOPIC: *Generosity*
SCRIPTURE: *Mark 12:41-44*
SUPPLIES: *large bag of candy*

Have teenagers form three groups. Give each person in the first group an equal number of candies—at least ten per person. Give each person in the second group five candies. Give the third group no candy.

Invite the groups to intermingle and mill about. Every time you clap, each person must give some of his or her candies to someone

JOBS LIST

Cashier at drive-through window

Baby sitter

Grocery store bagger

Missionary

Soup kitchen helper

Social worker

Pastor

Youth leader

Movie concessions worker

Radio announcer

Talk show host

Referee

Action movie star

Pop singer

Painter

Guitar player for rock band

School teacher

Banker

Secretary

Construction worker

else—not necessarily to someone who has no candy—based upon the number of times you clap. For example, if you clap twice, each person must give two pieces of candy to someone else. If you clap three times, each person must give three pieces of candy, and so on. If a person has no candy in hand, he or she gives nothing.

The object of the game is to see who ends up with the most pieces of candy.

DISCUSSION

• How did it feel to begin the game with no candy? lots of candy? some candy?
• How did this game reflect real life?
• What did it feel like to give up your candy? to receive candy from others?
• Read Mark 12:41-44. What does this Scripture passage teach about giving?
• Why is generosity sometimes difficult for us?
• How might generosity become a way of life?
• What can we do to make life more equitable for all people?

Shock Wave

TOPIC: *Compassion*
SCRIPTURE: *Ephesians 4:32*
SUPPLIES: *2 coins, 2 spoons*

Have teenagers form two equal teams. If you have an uneven number of people, join one of the teams to make them equal.

Have team members line up single file, sit on the floor, and hold hands. Give the person at the front of each line a coin. Place a spoon on the floor at the end of each line. All the players must look down at the floor or toward the ends of the lines where the spoons are. No one is allowed to look at the player with the coin.

When the game begins, the two people with the coins should begin tossing them. If a coin comes up "tails," nothing happens. If a coin comes up "heads," the person with the coin squeezes the hand of the next person in line, who squeezes the next person's hand,

and so on down the line to the last person, who grabs the spoon. After the person grabs the spoon, he or she drops the spoon, runs to the front of the line, and becomes the coin flipper. The old coin flipper becomes the second person in the line. The game continues until one team's original coin flipper ends up at the front of the line as the coin flipper again.

No one can squeeze a hand until his or her hand is squeezed first. If a team grabs the spoon illegally, that team is penalized—the coin flipper must go down to the end of the line. It's a good idea to station a referee at both ends of the lines to make sure everything is done legally.

DISCUSSION

• What made it difficult to wait to pass the shock wave down the line?
• Was it more difficult to be a person in line or to be a coin flipper? Why?
• How is this game similar to sharing compassion with others?
• What are some ways to show compassion?
• How can we begin to see ourselves as instruments of compassion in our world and to the body of Christ?

Sprint 'n' Swing!

TOPIC: *Popularity*
SCRIPTURE: *Matthew 7:13-14*
SUPPLIES: *warm, flat soda; ice water; cups*

Before the game, fill cups with warm, flat soda. You'll need one cup of soda per person.

Have everyone gather at one end of the playing area. Have participants form a single file line. Explain that on the signal, the first person in line is to quickly sprint to the other side of the room, touch the wall, and return, moving to the end of the line. Upon reaching the end of the line, the player must drink a cup of soda.

Play the game until everyone has had the chance to run.

Then have teenagers form two groups. Have each group form a line with players standing side by side. Have groups stand so the lines are facing each other. Ask players to grab the elbows of the people standing across from them, forming a sort of bridge between the two lines.

Ask one of the players at one end of the bridge to crawl across the human bridge. In the meantime, fill cups with ice water—one cup per person. Once the crawling player reaches the other side, give him or her a cup of ice water as a reward. Then have that person join the end of the bridge as the second player crosses the bridge.

Have players take turns crossing the bridge. Award a cup of ice water to everyone who successfully makes it across the bridge. Be sure to have everyone who crosses join the end of the bridge. You may want to gradually move the bridge across the room so players won't get bunched up at one end.

DISCUSSION

- Which was easier, sprinting back and forth across the room or crawling over a human bridge?
- How did it feel to successfully sprint across the room?
- How did it feel to successfully cross the bridge?
- Which reward was greater, a cup of warm, flat soda or ice cold water? Why?
- What are some things that seem great to some, but offer negative consequences down the road?
- What are some things that seem unpleasant to some, but offer great rewards down the road?
- Why do you think popularity is so important to some people?
- What are some things people do to try to gain popularity?
- How can we help one another make wise choices?

Startled Steps

TOPIC: *Peace*
SCRIPTURE: *Isaiah 26:3*
SUPPLIES: *blindfold*

Before the game, clear the furniture and other obstacles out of a large playing area. Be sure you have a clear path from one wall to another.

Choose one person to be "It". Blindfold this person, and take him or her to one side of the room. When the blindfold is in place, scatter the remaining players around the playing area.

When you give the signal, the blindfolded player should start moving slowly to the other side of the room. Tell the player that his or her goal is to simply touch the opposite wall as quickly as possible, while bumping into the fewest possible people along the way. You'll be keeping track of the person's time, and you'll add ten seconds for each person he or she bumps.

Remaining players should stand silent and motionless. Whenever the blindfolded person bumps another player, the seeing player must yell, "Boo!" Play continues until the blindfolded player reaches the other side of the room. At that point, calculate the person's time, adding ten seconds for each person he or she bumped.

Ask "It" to give the blindfold to another player and join the others as potential obstacles. When the new "It" is blindfolded, have that person cross the room, keeping track of the time and how many people he or she bumps along the way.

Have participants take turns until everyone has had a chance to cross the room. Determine who had the fastest time (with the number of bumps factored in).

DISCUSSION

• What was frustrating about this game?
• Did you find the people yelling, "boo" helpful or distracting?
• How could others have made this game easier for you?
• How was this game similar to the challenges we face in everyday life?
• Read Isaiah 26:3. How can God bring peace to our lives?
• What can we do to dwell in God's peace?

Stressed-Out Tug of War

TOPIC : *Stress*

SCRIPTURE : *Psalm 62*

SUPPLIES : *30 feet of rope, masking tape*

Before the game, cut the rope into six five-foot lengths. Tie the pieces together at one end of each piece. The resulting rope should look like this:

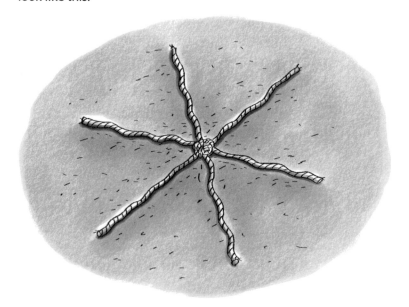

Lay the star-shaped rope out on the floor. Mark a masking tape line two feet behind the end of each point on the star.

Have teenagers form six equal teams. Have each team take a position behind one of the ropes. Ask the people on each team to number off from one on up, and remember their numbers.

To begin the game, call out a number. The people on each team who have been assigned that number will grab onto their ropes. When you say "go," all six people should pull. The first person to pull the rope over that team's masking tape line scores a point for the team. Continue until all the numbers have been called at least once.

DISCUSSION

- How did you feel when you were pulling on the rope?
- Was it more stressful pulling on the rope or waiting for your number to be called? Why?
- How was this tug of war similar to the stress we face in our everyday lives?
- How does waiting add unrealistic expectations and stress to our lives?
- How can reliance on God help us get a perspective on these areas of our lives?
- What unrealistic expectations do you place on yourself?
- What can we do to modify our unrealistic expectations?

Tapehead

TOPIC: *Siblings*
SCRIPTURE: *Luke 10:38-42*
SUPPLIES: *pantyhose; scissors; 2 plastic hoops or at least 16 feet of rope; the same number of small items per team, such as 10 marbles per team, 30 paper clips per team, 12 cotton balls per team, 18 pieces of hard candy per team, 10 straws per team; masking tape; 2 rolls of duct tape*

Before the game, cut the legs off the pantyhose. At one end of the room, lay two plastic hoops on the floor, or create two circles on the floor with rope. Place the same collection of small items inside each hoop or rope circle. Use masking tape to mark a starting line at the other end of the room.

Have teenagers form two teams. Each team will designate two people on the team to be the "Tapeheads." Give each of the Tapeheads a pantyhose leg, and ask them to place the legs over their heads.

Next, give each team a roll of duct tape. Have each team cover its Tapeheads' heads with tape, like a mummy, with the sticky side of the tape facing out. Be sure the Tapeheads' eyes and noses aren't covered.

When both teams have wrapped their Tapeheads, explain that Tapeheads will take turns using their heads to collect items from the hoops or ropes you've set up at the other end of the room. Each Tapehead will need a partner to help him or her get to the other end of the room. The Tapehead must walk on his or her hands while the partner carries Tapehead's feet, as in a wheelbarrow race.

When they reach the plastic hoop or rope circle, Tapehead's partner continues to hold Tapehead's feet. Tapehead must pick up articles with his or her head, without help from anyone else. When Tapehead has collected as much as possible in the first round, Tapehead and his or her partner will race back to the starting line, where the rest of the team will pluck the items off the person's head.

Once the first Tapehead returns to the starting line, the next Tapehead may take off with a partner and take a turn collecting items. This continues until you call time. Tally how many items each team collected, and congratulate students on their effort.

LEADER TIP

It's fun to play this game outdoors in the grass. Picking up the grass with your head adds to the challenge.

DISCUSSION

- How did cooperation between Tapehead, the partner, and the rest of the team add to your success in this game?
- How would this game have been different if you hadn't all worked together?
- Read Luke 10:38-42. When have you felt like Martha? When have you felt like Mary?
- Why is it important for siblings to get along with one another?
- What is your responsibility as a brother or sister?
- How do your choices influence your siblings?
- How can you become a better sibling?

Tear 'Em Apart

TOPIC: *Peace*
SCRIPTURE: *Philippians 4:4-7*
SUPPLIES: *none*

Have all the guys stand in the middle of the playing area, and have the girls stand around the edges of the room. Tell the guys to form a group and attach themselves to one another as tightly as they can. Tell the girls that their goal is to separate the guys from one another and drag them to the sides of the room. Once the girls separate a guy, he can't run back and reattach; he just has to let the girls drag him to the side of the room.

Give the guys time to form a tight group, and then allow the girls to attack. The game is over when all the guys are separated or when all the girls give up.

DISCUSSION

- Who do you think had more fun in that game, the girls or the guys? Why?
- Why do you think the game turned out the way it did?
- How did you feel while playing that game?
- When have you experienced those feelings in real life?

- What is peace?
- What do we need to feel at peace?
- What does it mean to have the peace of God?

Temptation on Your Shoulders

TOPIC: *Temptation*

SCRIPTURE: *1 Peter 1:13-16*

SUPPLIES: *photocopies of the "Temptation Cards" handout (p. 87), scissors, pins or tape, paper, pens or pencils*

Before the game, make enough photocopies of the "Temptation Cards" handout (p. 87) for each person to have one card. Cut apart the cards.

Without letting teenagers see what you're putting on their backs, pin or tape a card from the "Temptation Cards" handout on each person's back. Tell participants not to let other students know what is on their backs.

LEADER TIP
Do not assign a specific temptation to a person if you know that he or she actually struggles with it.

Give each person paper and a pen or pencil. Instruct players to walk around the room, silently reading the temptations on other people's backs. After reading the temptations, they should think of sincere advice for dealing with the temptations and write that advice on the other people's pieces of paper. Be sure players know that they should give their advice without giving away what the temptations are.

Continue the game until each person has at least five bits of advice on his or her paper. Then have each person guess what temptation is on his or her back. Tell the answers if people guess wrong, then have each person read aloud the advice on his or her paper.

DISCUSSION

- Read 1 Peter 1:13-16. Does the advice we gave one another fit with this Scripture?
- What does it mean to be self-controlled?
- What does it mean to be holy?
- How can we take advantage of God's power to deal with temptation?

TEMPTATION CARDS

I want to smoke pot with my friends.	**I get jealous of people who are popular and athletic.**
When I go into a store, I want to put things in my pockets and not pay for them.	**My friends swear so much that I find myself starting to do it too.**
I'm really curious to know what it would feel like to get really drunk.	**I hate getting into trouble with my folks. I think it might be best just to lie to them about where I've been.**
I'm really curious about pornography.	**I just met a really attractive person who is older. Maybe I should lie about my age.**
I'll fail my math class if I don't cheat on the final test.	**It doesn't seem to be a big deal to break the law by making copies of favorite CDs or movies.**

Testing! Testing!

TOPIC: *Temptation*

SCRIPTURE: *Matthew 6:13*

SUPPLIES: *slips of paper, pen or pencil, envelopes, hat or box*

Before the game, write the following temptations on slips of paper (create more if you have more than twenty people in your group). Place the slips of paper in envelopes (one per envelope), and seal the envelopes. Place the envelopes in a hat or box.

• Someone wants to sell you a stolen pager—cheap!

• You can make an A in algebra—if you copy from the class brain.

• Your friends want to view some porn sites on the Web.

• You forgot to call your girlfriend/boyfriend—but you can always lie!

• You'd like to fight it out with a school bully—why not?

• You don't want to work, so you call in sick—what's wrong with that?

• You want to dump your girlfriend/boyfriend, so you're acting mean—isn't that OK?

• You found a wallet with several twenties—can you take just one?

• You can get into a concert for free—if you crawl under the fence.

• Someone called you a name—but you've got a great comeback.

Have teenagers form two teams. Each team must send one person to the middle of the room for a one-on-one competition.

Invite someone to draw one of the temptations from the hat and read it aloud. Each person in the middle then has one minute to offer a response to the temptation. Following the responses, each team should confer briefly and offer a consensus score of one to ten to reflect how well they believe the person on the other team responded to the question. The score should reflect how well the person on the other team answered based upon Christian values and beliefs.

Play until each person has had an opportunity to be in the middle. The team with the highest score wins.

DISCUSSION

• Which descriptions seem especially tempting? Why?

• What are some other possible responses to various temptations?

• How might God help us when temptations present themselves?

- What are some ways we might guard ourselves from the power of temptation?
- What do you think are some of the most powerful temptations for teenagers today?
- What hope is there for those who fail or fall into sin?

This Little Light of Mine

TOPIC: *Sharing Faith*

SCRIPTURE: *Matthew 5:14-16*

SUPPLIES: *1 small flashlight or penlight per player, a dark building*

Before the meeting, make sure you can completely darken the playing area. This is a great variation on Hide and Seek for lock-ins or anytime when you have the whole building to yourself.

Give each person a small flashlight or penlight. Choose a volunteer to be "It". Instruct everyone else to go and hide somewhere in the building (or within the boundaries you've established). Players can't hide with anyone else and shouldn't try to see where other people hide. Players should keep their flashlights or penlights turned off.

After two or three minutes, allow "It" to turn on his or her light, and send "It" out to find other players. When "It" finds a hiding player, the newly found player lights his or her flashlight or penlight and helps "It" look for others.

Each time a player is found, that person should turn on his or her light and become part of the seeking team. When all the players have been found and have turned on their lights, choose a new "It" and play another round.

DISCUSSION

- Read Matthew 5:14-16. How did the game we just played illustrate this Scripture?
- What is the light this Scripture refers to?
- What are some of the ways our society can put out the light?
- What are some of the ways we put the light out ourselves?
- What are some specific ways we can share the light with others?

Touchy

TOPIC: *Body Image*
SCRIPTURE: *Matthew 6:25-29*
SUPPLIES: *1 blindfold per group of 6 to 8*

Have teenagers form groups of six to eight. Give each group a blindfold, and have one person in each group put on the blindfold.

To begin the game, call out one part of the body from the list below.

- Hair
- Ear
- Elbow
- Forearm
- Knee
- Toe
- Hand
- Ankle

Have one person stand in front of the person wearing the blindfold. Have another person pick up the hand of the blindfolded person and place it on the designated part of the other person. The blindfolded person should try to guess who he or she is touching. If the guess is correct, the guesser gets to give the blindfold to the other person. If the guess is incorrect, the guesser must keep the blindfold on for the next round.

Have another person stand in front of the guesser, and call out another body part from the list. Continue the game until everyone has had a chance to be blindfolded.

DISCUSSION

- Read Matthew 6:25-29. In what ways do people worry too much about their bodies? Why?
- How does God want us to feel about our bodies? Explain.
- How do you think God sees your body?
- When you were blindfolded, did people feel similar or different?
- Do you think God desires for us to all look similar or different? Why?
- What can we learn from thinking about birds and flowers, as the Scripture passage suggests?

Truly Trivial Trivia

TOPIC: *Media*

SCRIPTURE: *James 4:4*

SUPPLIES: *photocopies of the "Truly Trivial Trivia Questions" handout (p. 92)*

Have teenagers form groups of four to six. Give each person a photocopy of the "Truly Trivial Trivia Questions" handout (p. 92). See which group can answer the questions the fastest. If no group knows all the answers, see which group can fill in the most answers.

See the chart below for the answers to the questions on the handout.

ANSWERS TO TRULY TRIVIAL TRIVIA QUESTIONS

This quotation is from what movie? "Go ahead, make my day." **Answer: Sudden Impact**	This quotation is from what movie? "Here's Johnny!" **Answer: The Shining**	This quotation is from what movie? "They're here." **Answer: Poltergeist**
On *I Love Lucy*, what was Lucy Ricardo's maiden name? **Answer: MacGillicuddy**	What was Mr. Howell's full name on *Gilligan's Island*? **Answer: Thurston Howell III**	What was the last name of the Ricardos' landlords on *I Love Lucy*? **Answer: Mertz**
This quotation is from what movie? "Mrs. Robinson, you're trying to seduce me." **Answer: The Graduate**	This quotation is from what movie? "Hasta la vista, baby." **Answer: Terminator 2: Judgment Day**	This quotation is from what movie? "Here's looking at you, kid." **Answer: Casablanca**
This quotation is from what movie? "Life is like a box of chocolates; you never know what you're gonna get." **Answer: Forrest Gump**	This quotation is from what movie? "I'll be back." **Answer: The Terminator**	This quotation is from what movie? "Phone home." **Answer: E.T.**
What were the names of the two actors who played Darrin on *Bewitched*? **Answer: Dick York and Dick Sargent**	What was the name of Alice's boyfriend on *The Brady Bunch*? **Answer: Sam**	What was the name of the van on *Scooby-Doo, Where Are You!*? **Answer: The Mystery Machine**
This quotation is from what movie? "I don't know nothin' 'bout birthin' babies." **Answer: Gone With the Wind**	This quotation is from what movie? "Love means never having to say you're sorry." **Answer: Love Story**	This quotation is from what movie? "Toto, I've a feeling we're not in Kansas anymore." **Answer: The Wizard of Oz**

TRULY TRIVIAL TRIVIA QUESTIONS

This quotation is from what movie? "Go ahead, make my day."	This quotation is from what movie? "Here's Johnny!"	This quotation is from what movie? "They're here."
On *I Love Lucy*, what was Lucy Ricardo's maiden name?	What was Mr. Howell's full name on *Gilligan's Island*?	What was the last name of the Ricardos' landlords on *I Love Lucy*?
This quotation is from what movie? "Mrs. Robinson, you're trying to seduce me."	This quotation is from what movie? "Hasta la vista, baby."	This quotation is from what movie? "Here's looking at you, kid."
This quotation is from what movie? "Life is like a box of chocolates; you never know what you're gonna get."	This quotation is from what movie? "I'll be back."	This quotation is from what movie? "Phone home."
What were the names of the two actors who played Darrin on *Bewitched*?	What was the name of Alice's boyfriend on *The Brady Bunch*?	What was the name of the van on *Scooby-Doo, Where Are You!*?
This quotation is from what movie? "I don't know nothin' 'bout birthin' babies."	This quotation is from what movie? "Love means never having to say you're sorry."	This quotation is from what movie? "Toto, I've a feeling we're not in Kansas anymore."

- How did your group know the answers to these questions?
- How do you feel about how much television you watch each week? how many movies you attend in a month?
- Would you say that all these movies or shows would be pleasing to God? Why or why not?
- How do television and movies influence people?
- How can we make sure we're living a balanced life and spending our time on things that are important?

Turban Tag

TOPIC: *Unity*
SCRIPTURE: *Philippians 2:1-11*
SUPPLIES: *1 towel per person*

Give each person a towel, and instruct players to wrap the towels securely around their heads like turbans. Explain that there are no teams in this game. Everyone should try to knock the turbans off the heads of opponents while protecting the turban on his or her own head. When a person's turban is knocked off, that person is out of the game.

LEADER TIP

Allow participants to use their hands in the first few rounds, but later, for an extra challenge, try a round with no hands.

If necessary, remind players to be careful and not to hit other people. The winner is the last person with a turban on his or her head.

DISCUSSION

• How would this game have been different if we had played as teams instead of individuals?
• What was everyone's common goal in this game?
• What is our common goal as Christians?
• How can we work together as a team to fulfill our mission?
• Read Philippians 2:1-11 aloud. According to these verses, how can we go about achieving unity?
• What can we learn from Christ's example?
• What would you consider the greatest threats to unity?
• Can you share a time you put someone else's needs ahead of your own?
• What benefits can we enjoy by working toward this sort of unselfish attitude in our group?

Two-by-Two Race

TOPIC: *Creation*
SCRIPTURE: *Genesis 1:1-27*
SUPPLIES: *masking tape*

Have teenagers form two teams. Have teams stand on opposite sides of the room. Use masking tape to mark a line in front of each team, and mark a line in the middle of the room that is of equal distance from both teams.

Have one person from each team begin the race to the tape in the middle of the room by acting like a certain animal. For example, you might tell the first person on each team to act like a donkey. The two people might walk on all fours and bray and kick as they race to the middle and back to their team. You might tell the second person on each team to act like a duck. Continue calling out specific animals as people take turns racing to and from the middle of the room. Other ideas for animals include a cat, a pig, a cow, a turtle, an elephant, and a monkey. Challenge the teams to try to complete the race as fast as they can.

DISCUSSION

• What are some of the differences between us and the animals God created?
• Read Genesis 1:1-27. Do you believe God created the world? Why or why not?
• What other Bible passages support God's creation of the world?
• How are we created in God's image?

Two Left Hands

TOPIC: *Love*
SCRIPTURE: *1 Corinthians 13:13; Galatians 5:22-23*
SUPPLIES: *1 banana per pair, 1 orange per pair, variety of other fruits, chairs, blindfolds*

Have participants form pairs. One person from each pair should sit in a chair while that person's partner stands behind the chair. Every seated person should be blindfolded.

The person standing up will lend his or her left hand to the person sitting down. The person sitting down can use only his or her left hand, so each sitting person has the use of two left hands.

Give each pair a banana and an orange, and distribute any other fruit evenly among pairs. When the contest begins, each pair must peel the banana and the orange and any other fruit with its two left hands. The person standing up must feed all the fruit to the person sitting down. Pairs should try to eat all their fruit as quickly as possible.

DISCUSSION

• What was the most difficult part of this game? Why?
• How did you make your partnership work to accomplish your task?
• How were the partnerships in this game similar to relationships in real life?
• How does love change people's lives?
• Read Galatians 5:22-23. How do we become loving people?
• Read 1 Corinthians 13:13. Why do you think God values love more than anything?

Two Thumbs, Way Up

TOPIC: *Media*
SCRIPTURE: *Philippians 4:8*
SUPPLIES: *Hula-Hoop, watch with a second hand*

Place the Hula-Hoop in the middle of the room. Position teenagers in a circle around the Hula-Hoop. Explain that this game requires quick reactions, great timing, and an encyclopedic knowledge of movies.

Here's what teenagers will do: When inspiration strikes, someone will jump into the Hula-Hoop and deliver a line from a movie. It's most effective if the line is delivered in character. For instance, a teenager may leap into the Hula-Hoop and, with a Bogart-inspired sneer, say, "Here's lookin' at you, kid." The rest of the teenagers will guess until someone identifies the correct movie title (*Casablanca*).

Explain that the goal is to correctly guess as many movies as possible in ninety-seven seconds. Tell students that only one person is allowed in the Hula-Hoop at a time. If nobody guesses a particular title in ten seconds, then that effort can be abandoned and another student can jump in the Hula-Hoop and say a line. Make sure students say only one line, but let them know that actions can be used as well.

Play several rounds, challenging the students to improve upon the number of movies guessed in previous rounds.

DISCUSSION

- Why are movie characters and dialogues so often memorable?
- What would have happened to this game if we'd been restricted to films that honor God?
- What makes a particular film appropriate or inappropriate for a Christian to view?

Unwarranted Wetness

TOPIC: *Justice*

SCRIPTURE: *Revelation 11:18*

SUPPLIES: *2 large containers such as garbage cans, 3 water balloons per person*

Note: This game should be played outside.

Before the game, fill three water balloons per person. Place one balloon per person in a large container such as a garbage can. Label that container "A." Put the remaining balloons in the other container, and label that container "B." Place the containers at opposite ends of the playing area.

Have teenagers form two teams, and designate one Team A and the other Team B. Explain that teams will be participating in a water balloon competition to see which team can stay the driest. Show teams the boundaries for the competition, and point out the containers of water balloons. Explain that each team may take water balloons only from its own container, and all players must stay within the boundaries.

Don't reveal that one container has more balloons than the other—start the competition and let players figure it out for themselves. Continue play until all the water balloons have been broken, narrowing the boundaries if necessary to keep the game lively. Determine a winner based on which team, as a whole, is the driest (most likely Team B).

DISCUSSION

- Team A, how did you feel when you realized that Team B had been given more balloons?
- How is this game similar to the injustice in our world?
- What are some various kinds of injustice in our world?
- What are some ways you've seen justice triumph?
- How does it make you feel to know that in the end of all time, God will bring perfect justice to all?

Wandering Evil

TOPIC: *Evil*

SCRIPTURE: *Proverbs 1:10-15*

SUPPLIES: *slips of paper, marker*

Before the game, place a mark on one slip of paper that will be obvious to the person who draws it, then fold the slips of paper so students won't be able to see which paper has the mark on it.

Have teenagers stand in a circle. Explain that you're going to distribute slips of paper. Ask students not to look at their slips until you give the signal. After you've passed out the slips of paper, allow students to look at their slips, but ask them not to look at anyone else's.

Tell the person who got the slip with the mark on it to avoid letting anyone else know. That person is "It." Explain that "It's" job will be to destroy people by touching them as everyone walks around the room in silence.

Have players begin walking around the room, and instruct "It" to touch people inconspicuously. If someone is touched, that person should let out a loud scream and fall to the ground. Other players should try to figure out who "It" is.

Tell players that if they think they know who "It" is, they can raise their hands and ask to take a guess. If the guess is correct, start the game over by redistributing the slips of paper. If the guess is wrong, the person who guessed is out of the game.

DISCUSSION

- How was "It" in this game similar to evil in our world?
- What does evil look like?
- How can you know if something is evil?
- What does God say about evil things?
- What makes something evil?
- How does evil destroy us?
- How should we respond to evil?

We Are Family

TOPIC: *Family*
SCRIPTURE: *Genesis 25:24-34*
SUPPLIES: *2 foam balls of different colors or sizes*

Have everyone form a circle. (If you have a large group, have teenagers form groups of ten to fifteen and have each group form its own circle.) Give the foam balls to two people in the circle.

Encourage teenagers to get the feel of passing the balls around the circle to the left, then to the right. After a minute or so, begin the game. Everyone in the circle must pass one ball (designate which color or size) to the right. The other ball, however, can be thrown across the circle. Whenever someone has both balls at the same time, that person must say something affirming about the people on his or her left and right. Then have teenagers begin passing and tossing the balls again.

Continue play until most, or all, people have had an opportunity to say something about others in the circle.

DISCUSSION

- In what ways did this game help us to appreciate one another better?
- Why do you think it can be difficult for us to affirm the people in our families?

- How might affirming our family members help us appreciate them better?
- Read Genesis 25:24-34. What kinds of difficulties did this family face?
- What difficulties do families face today?
- What makes you appreciate the people in your family?
- How can we improve relationships in our families?

What Goes Around...

TOPIC: *Evil*
SCRIPTURE: *Psalm 7:14-16*
SUPPLIES: *balls of various sizes and types (such as baseballs, rubber balls, soccer balls, foam balls, volleyballs, and super balls)*

Have teenagers stand in a circle. Tell them that they're going to throw a ball around the circle. Each person should receive the ball only once. The last person to receive the ball should be the first one who threw it. Tell players to remember who they received the ball from and who they threw it to.

After the ball has made one full trip around the circle, play again to be sure the pattern is the same. Then on the third trip around the circle, add a second ball, copying the pattern exactly. Try again, adding a third ball. See how many different balls you can keep flying around the circle until it gets too chaotic.

DISCUSSION

- Have you ever heard the phrase "What goes around comes around"? What does it mean?
- Read Psalm 7:14-16. How do you think this Scripture applies to the game we just played?
- Have you ever told a lie to someone and then had to continually juggle to support it? What happened?
- Why does it seem like the bad guys win so often?
- If we live our lives causing trouble, how might it come back to us?
- What happens when we try to make the world a better place?

What's Eating You?

TOPIC: *Unity*
SCRIPTURE: *Ephesians 4:11-16*
SUPPLIES: *many varieties of chewing gum*

Have each person select a piece of gum and hold on to it. Have youth form groups of five or six. When you say "go," each person should quickly unwrap the piece of gum and begin chewing. Each person should chew and make a bubble as quickly as possible, being careful not to let the bubble pop. The winner is the first group in which all members have intact bubbles. Some youth will take longer because they didn't choose bubble gum, but the game will work with all types of gum.

DISCUSSION

- What made this game more difficult for some than for others?
- In what ways does God use people who have different gifts to accomplish the same goals?
- How can we learn to work together, using individual gifts and talents to become unified in our goal to glorify God?
- In what ways does being unified protect us against the schemes of the devil?

- How does the saying "There is strength in numbers" relate to unity?
- How does unity as a group affect us as individuals?

Who Is That?

TOPIC: *The Bible*

SCRIPTURE: *2 Timothy 3:16-17; James 1:22-25*

SUPPLIES: *paper, pens or pencils, blindfolds*

Give each person paper, a pen or pencil, and a blindfold. After each player is blindfolded, have teenagers write down the answers to the following questions:

- What color are your socks?
- What color is your shirt?
- What is distinctive about the outfit you're wearing?

After everyone has written answers to the questions, have players turn over their papers, keeping the blindfolds on, and draw pictures of themselves. Give participants five minutes to create self-portraits. Then post all the pictures and see who did the best job.

DISCUSSION:

- What was it like to answer the three questions?
- What made it difficult to draw a picture of yourself?
- Read James 1:22-25. What does this Scripture say about the Bible?
- Why is it sometimes hard to do what the Bible says?
- Why do you think we tend to follow some Bible passages and ignore others?
- Read 2 Timothy 3:16-17. What do these verses say about ignoring certain parts of Scripture?
- How has the Bible affected your life?

Wise Up

TOPIC: *Wisdom*

SCRIPTURE: *Proverbs 2:1-6*

SUPPLIES: *index cards, pen or pencil*

Before the game, write the following statements on index cards (one statement per card). You may want to create your own statements, too.

- I picked up a bee, got stung, and learned…
- I drove my car too fast, wrecked it, and learned…
- I helped a neighbor and learned…
- I was showing off for someone and learned…
- I spent all my money and learned…

Have teenagers form two teams. Give teams an equal number of the index cards you prepared beforehand. Invite someone on each team to read a situation aloud and complete the thought. The other team must then assign a score for the response: between one and ten points.

After all the cards have been used, see which team has the highest score.

DISCUSSION

- Which responses were particularly wise or insightful?
- How is wisdom different from knowledge?
- What are some of the positive rewards for using wisdom?
- Read Proverbs 2:1-6. How can we go about finding God's wisdom? Where is God's wisdom found?
- What's one piece of wisdom you've learned?

Work of Art

TOPIC: *Relationships*

SCRIPTURE: *Colossians 3:12-14*

SUPPLIES: *craft supplies (such as construction paper in various colors, scissors, glue or tape, toothpicks, newspaper, cardboard, cotton balls, and buttons)*

Using a variety of craft supplies, create your own unique and somewhat intricate work of art that can't be easily duplicated (or have another adult who likes art create the work of art). Be sure your creation involves different colors in different places; maybe even create something three-dimensional. Keep your artwork in a separate room where teenagers won't see it.

Have teenagers form teams of four to six people, and give each team all the items necessary to replicate your artwork, plus some additional items you didn't use to add confusion. Explain that one member of each team will have twenty seconds to run into the other room, study the artwork, and return to the team to give instructions on how to replicate it. The team member who observed the artwork isn't allowed to participate in constructing the artwork.

When the team reaches a dead end, they should send a new team member in to study the artwork for twenty seconds. That person then guides the team in replicating the artwork and is disqualified from participating in the creative process.

Teams should repeat the process until only one person is left to replicate the artwork and the team has reached a dead end. After all teams have finished this process, bring out the original artwork and let students see how closely their teams replicated it.

DISCUSSION

• What made this game easy or difficult?
• Who had an easier time giving instructions, the first team member or the last? Why?
• Was it easier to criticize or encourage your team members in this game? Why?
• What made your team successful or unsuccessful?
• How did this game illustrate the intricacy of relationships?
• According to God's Word, what makes relationships successful?

Worship Match-Up

TOPIC: *Worship*

SCRIPTURE: *Psalm 145:3; Revelation 4:11*

SUPPLIES: *photocopies of the "Descriptions of God" handout (p. 106); scissors; paper sacks; the following collection of objects for each team: ring, ruler, baby doll, building block, silk flower, bar of soap, hand weight, eraser, watch, candle, pillow, map, newspaper, bottle of water (you can substitute other objects if necessary—see below)*

Before the game, make a photocopy of the "Descriptions of God" handout (p. 106) for each team of up to ten people. Fill a paper sack for each team with the collection of objects.

Have teenagers form teams of no more than ten. Give each group a sack of objects, a photocopy of the "Descriptions of God" handout, and a pair of scissors. When you give the signal, teams should cut apart the descriptions on their handouts, open their sacks, and race to match each object with the description of God it represents. Once all of the teams have finished, have students take turns sharing why they matched each object and description. Once they've finished this, reveal the correct answers.

The correct matches are as follows (you can substitute other symbolic objects if necessary):

Faithful: ring
Ruler: ruler
Loving: baby doll
Creator: building block
Beautiful: silk flower
Righteous: bar of soap
Strong: hand weight
Forgiving: eraser
Eternal: watch
Light: candle
Peaceful: pillow
Omnipresent: map
Communicating: newspaper
Life-Giving: bottle of water

DESCRIPTIONS OF GOD

Cut apart the descriptions of God and match them
with the objects that best symbolize them.

Faithful

Ruler

Loving

Creator

Beautiful

Righteous

Strong

Forgiving

Eternal

Light

Peaceful

Omnipresent

Communicating

Life-Giving

DISCUSSION

- What valuable insights can we find in matches that weren't necessarily the "correct" answers?
- How have you experienced these descriptions of God in your life?
- What are some other qualities you appreciate about God?
- How would you define worship?
- What is your mental and emotional response to reminders of these characteristics of God?
- How can you worship God for his character and attributes?

INDEXES

JUMPSTARTERS

Group Publishing, Inc.
Attention: Product Development
P.O. Box 481
Loveland, CO 80539
Fax: (970) 679-4370

Evaluation for
JumpStarters: 100 Games to Spark Discussion

Please help Group Publishing, Inc. continue to provide innovative and useful resources for ministry. Please take a moment to fill out this evaluation and mail or fax it to us. Thanks!

● ● ●

1. As a whole, this book has been (circle one)

not very helpful   very helpful

1   2   3   4   5   6   7   8   9   10

2. The best things about this book:

3. Ways this book could be improved:

4. Things I will change because of this book:

5. Other books I'd like to see Group publish in the future:

6. Would you be interested in field-testing future Group products and giving us your feedback? If so, please fill in the information below:

Name_____

Church Name _____

Denomination _____ Church Size _____

Church Address _____

City   State   ZIP

Church Phone _____

E-mail _____

Exciting Resources for Your Youth Ministry

At Risk: Bringing Hope to Hurting Teenagers

Dr. Scott Larson .

Discover how to meet the needs of hurting teenagers with these practical suggestions, honest answers, and tools to help you evaluate your existing programs. Plus, you'll get real-life insights about what it takes to include kids others have left behind. If you believe the Gospel is for everyone, this book is for you! Includes a special introduction by Duffy Robbins and a foreword by Dean Borgman.

ISBN 0-7644-2091-7

All-Star Games From All-Star Youth Leaders

The ultimate game book—from the biggest names in youth ministry! All-time no-fail favorites from Wayne Rice, Les Christie, Rich Mullins, Tiger McLuen, Darrell Pearson, Dave Stone, Bart Campolo, Steve Fitzhugh, and 21 others! You get all the games you'll need for any situation. Plus, you get practical advice about how to design your own games and tricks for turning a *good* game into a *great* game!

ISBN 0-7644-2020-8

The Youth Worker's Encyclopedia of Bible-Teaching Ideas

Here are the most comprehensive idea-books available for youth workers. With more than 365 creative ideas in each of these 400-page encyclopedias, there's at least one idea for every book of the Bible. You'll find ideas for retreats and overnighters...learning games...adventures...projects...affirmations...parties... prayers...music...devotions...skits...and more!

Old Testament ISBN 1-55945-184-X
New Testament ISBN 1-55945-183-1

Awesome Worship Services for Youth

These 12 complete worship services involve kids in 4 key elements of worship: celebration, reflection, symbolic action, and declaration of God's Truth. Flexible and dynamic services each last about an hour and will bring your group closer to God.

ISBN 0-7644-2057-7